Sunset

ideas for great WINDOW TREATMENTS

By Christine Barnes, Susan Lang,
and the Editors of Sunset Books

Sunset Books ■ Menlo Park, California

Sunset Books

vice president, general manager:
Richard A. Smeby

editorial director, vice president:
Bob Doyle

production director:
Lory Day

art director:
Vasken Guiragossian

Staff for this book:

developmental editor:
Linda J. Selden

copy editor:
Marcia Williamson

design:
Barbara Vick

page layout:
Kathy Avanzino Barone

illustrations:
Beverly Colgan
Sally Shimizu

principal photographer:
E. Andrew McKinney

photo director/stylist:
JoAnn Masaoka Van Atta

production coordinator:
Patricia S. Williams

10 9 8 7

First printing January 2000

ISBN 0-376-01756-2
Library of Congress Catalog Card Number: 99-60453
Printed in the United States.

For additional copies of Ideas for Great Window Treatments or any other Sunset Book, call 1-800-526-5111.
Or see our web site at: www.sunsetbooks.com

Cover: Balloon shades made of natural silk blend with neutral walls and furnishings in an understated scheme. Mounting the treatments at the ceiling accentuates tall windows. Interior design by Steven Shubel. Cover design by Vasken Guiragossian. Photography by Alan Weintraub/Arcaid.

The new simplicity

Have you noticed? There's a new attitude in the world of window treatments. Time-honored coverings are still available and often appropriate, but many of today's styles are sleek and simple, and much of the latest hardware has gone high-tech. A quiet revolution has occurred in window fashions, and the current look might best be described as "the new simplicity."

Achieving this look is not as difficult as it might seem. On the following pages you'll find guidelines for choosing the best treatments for your windows, as well as help with color and design decisions. A gallery of window treatments displays the range of possibilities, from classic to innovative. Turn to the shopping guide for help in selecting the most suitable products.

Many individuals and firms assisted in the planning of this book, and you will find their names in the credits on pages 110–111. We'd especially like to thank Calico Corners, Juliana Edlund, Kathy Harding of Harding & Racz Interiors, Joan Osburn, Kim Smith of Young's Interiors, and Karen Winger.

contents

special features

window dressing

What would we do without windows? They allow welcome light and air into our homes, expand the sense of interior spaciousness, and frame our view of the world beyond. Windows are nothing short of wonderful!

But for all their benefits, windows present more than a few aesthetic and practical challenges. Uncovered, they admit harsh sun, passing glances, and chilling drafts. Bare windows can also appear cold and unfinished unless they're architecturally noteworthy or located where privacy and light control are not concerns. The latter situation is a luxury, however, and for both beauty and function, most windows need window treatments. How to dress your windows, from idea to installation, is what this book is about.

If you think your options are few—a café curtain, a metal miniblind, a pinch-pleated drapery—you are in for a big, and pleasant, surprise. Familiar styles are still available, of course—rod-pocket curtains, tailored Roman shades, plantation shutters, to name a few. And many old favorites are open to fresh interpretations, such as new patterned sheers attached to sleek hardware, or panels that sport innovative pleats. For pared-down decorating schemes, you'll find a wealth of blinds, shades, and shutters in all sorts of colors and finishes.

Settling on a window-treatment style is only part of the process. Once upon a time (in the '50s and before), the only decision was whether to go with beige or ivory antique satin for the living room "drapes." That attitude has evolved, fortunately, and today's

window coverings are an integral part of a decorating plan, not an afterthought.

To give window treatments their due, formulate a few decorating goals: Do you hope to create a high-energy, high-contrast room, where the window treatments take center stage? Or, do you lean toward supporting-role treatments that blend and harmonize with other furnishings? How do you see color and pattern at your windows—and throughout the room? These may sound like difficult questions, but design decisions are creative and fun, and clear goals can help you achieve a pleasing outcome.

There's no doubt about it: today's windows wear an astonishing array of window fashions. With a little planning and shopping, you can find that just-right treatment and add your windows to the best-dressed list.

A PLANNING PRIMER

GRACEFUL SWAGS, relaxed panels, hard-working blinds—behind every winning window treatment is a careful plan, one that suits both the design of your window and the style of your home. If you're not quite sure how to formulate that plan, this chapter will help. START WITH a style-by-style overview of the possibilities. Then take up color and design considerations, including how to choose coverings that blend into a scheme or command attention. Functional matters count, too; light control, privacy, and safety concerns are just as important as design decisions. Finally, see how different treatment styles look on 11 types of windows. SOME WINDOWS are easy to handle; others are a real challenge. But almost without exception, you have a variety of pleasing and practical choices. Start making plans!

window wear

One look *at a decorating magazine will convince you that there's been an explosion in window coverings and their hardware in recent years. To help you make the best choices, look through the following pages to see what today's windows are wearing.*

Rod-pocket curtains are among the most versatile window-treatment styles, adapting as well to tailored fabrics as to feminine ones.

Curtains

The word "curtains" once conjured up images of cheerful cafés or ruffled, crisscross Priscillas. Not anymore. Curtains now come in a wide—and sometimes confusing—range of styles, from sleek and simple to voluminous and structured. Following are the most popular options.

By definition, curtains are panels of fabric gathered onto a rod or attached to it by tabs, ties, clips, or rings. Depending on the width of the panels and the hardware used, curtains can appear full or almost flat. Curtains are sometimes called "draperies," although, strictly speaking, they are not. Draperies are attached to a traverse rod, and you open and close them by means of a cord or wand; if the panels open and close by hand, they are curtains.

Rod-pocket curtains. This well-known curtain style features a stitched pocket that gathers onto a rod; designers sometimes describe rod-pocket curtains as "shirred on a rod." If there's extra fabric above the pocket, a ruffle (called the heading) forms when the panel is gathered. A rod-pocket curtain gathered at both top and bottom is called a sash or hourglass curtain; one that covers the lower half of the window, ending at the sill or below the window frame, is a café.

Rod-pocket curtains are by nature stationary—it's difficult to pull them over the rod—so plan to use them in situations where they will remain in place. The panels may be scooped to the side and held back with tiebacks or holdbacks, or they may hang free.

Flat curtain panels. A simple, popular alternative to rod-pocket curtains, "flat" curtains

Shimmery textured fabrics lend themselves to flat curtain panels. Distinctive hardware is a good choice for simple treatments.

Crinkly curtains are clipped to metal rings on wire "rods." Spacing the clips widely allows the panel to droop casually.

have some fullness, though less than gathered styles. Flat panels are often made of cotton and linen fabrics, but some of the most elegant window treatments consist of silk panels hanging from decorative rings on ornate rods.

Pleated curtains. Is there such a thing as a pleated curtain? Yes, but the difference between a pleated curtain and a pleated drapery is not always obvious. Pleated panels attached to rings or clips are still curtains if they open and close by hand. Confusion arises because pleated draperies on decorative traverse rods (these also have rings) can look just like pleated curtains on rings, and vice versa. You often can't tell until you look up and under the panels to see the hardware. Most of the pleated treatments shown in decorating books and magazines are in fact curtains. (For pleat styles, see pages 10 and 11.)

Linings were once a standard component of curtains, but times have changed, and many curtain panels, especially ready-made ones, are now unlined. That's fine if your room is casual or you prefer a sheer fabric and an airy effect, but review the benefits of linings (page 87) before making a decision.

Keeping Tabs

Tab curtains—panels with tabs, loops, or ties at the heading—never go out of style, in part because they adapt easily to a wide variety of windows and window-treatment hardware, even whimsical "twig" poles. Fabrics range from nubby cottons to plush velvets.

Most tabs are stitched into the heading of the curtain panel, concealing the ends, or lapped over the heading and topstitched. The latter treatment is often punctuated by a button at the base of each tab. Other variations include tabs that are cinched at the base and tabs made of thin cording or flat braid. Tied tabs form chunky knots if the tabs are short and wide, or drape gracefully over the rod if the tabs are long and slender.

Keep in mind that some curtains with tabs, bows, or knots do not move easily, if at all. Plan to use them primarily as stationary panels, perhaps in combination with a functional shade or blind.

Slim tabs

Topstitched tabs

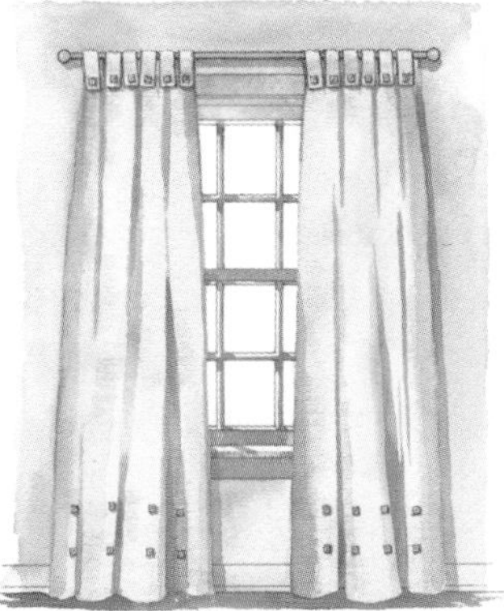

Square-button tabs

Tied tabs

Pinch-pleated draperies made of silk are an elegant and practical solution for a bow window. The custom-bent rod was painted to blend with the wall color.

Draperies

What was once the mainstay of window fashions—the pinch-pleated drapery—has evolved into a collection of designs with imaginative and innovative pleats. As with curtains, the heading sets the style and mood.

Draperies are pleated panels hanging from hooks that attach to small slides on a standard or decorative traverse rod (see page 91). You open and close the panels by a cord that moves the slides along a track.

Whether you choose a standard traverse rod, which is covered by the top of the pleated panels, or a decorative traverse rod, which is always exposed, depends on the style of your room and the drapery fabric. Standard traverse rods are traditional; decorative models can work in both traditional and contemporary schemes.

Your options in pleats include both classic and current looks.

Pinch pleat. This traditional pleat, which has largely been replaced by newer styles, consists of a loop of fabric that's folded into three shallow pleats and tacked at the base; the pleats repeat at intervals across the panel. Crinoline (a 4-inch band of stiffener) stitched inside the heading keeps the pleats crisp. For a more contemporary look, tack the pleats farther up the crinoline. If you like the practicality of draperies but don't care for pinch pleats, consider combining pleated panels with a valance or cornice that conceals the heading.

French pleat. Although it's formed much like a pinch pleat, a French pleat features softer, less defined folds.

Reverse pinch pleat. The loop of fabric for a reverse pinch pleat is folded around, to the sides, and tacked at the base for a smooth, rounded heading.

Fan pleat. Sometimes referred to as a waterfall pleat, this style consists of three folds of fabric, but they are tacked at the top, so that the fullness "fans" down and slightly outward. The absence of crinoline in the heading gives a fan pleat its soft, unstructured look. Extra distance between the pleats creates a free-hanging panel that droops casually at intervals on the floor.

Goblet pleat. Perhaps the most formal and sophisticated of the pleat styles, a goblet pleat is formed by tucking or cinching the loop of fabric at the base rather than folding it, forming a cylinder. Crinoline in the heading maintains the shape of the pleats; a newer version, without the crinoline, is less structured. Panels with goblet pleats are not, technically speaking, draperies because they must be stationary—opening them would crush the pleats.

Cartridge pleat. Smaller than a goblet pleat, a cartridge pleat consists of a loop, usually 1 inch to 1½ inches in diameter, that is neither folded nor cinched. A small piece of crinoline slipped inside each loop helps maintain the shape of the pleats.

Pencil pleat. Even smaller than a cartridge pleat, this style is achieved with pleating tape sewn to the back of the panel at the upper edge. Cords inside the tape allow you to gather the heading into narrow, uniform pleats.

Butterfly pleat. Also known as a two-finger pleat, this style features two folds rather than three. A butterfly pleat uses less fabric and is considered more casual than a pinch pleat.

Box pleat. This deep, inverted pleat is another style that's suitable only for stationary panels or valances, not traversing draperies. Because they require firm support, box-pleated panels must be attached to a board.

Pleats with extra folds of fabric flare at the top. Hooks inserted behind the pleats attach to rings.

When tacked at the very base of the crinoline (the stiffener), pinch pleats become long and sleek, an appropriate style for iridescent silk panels.

Three small tucks form the characteristic shape of a goblet pleat.

Stitched Roman shades (with dowels inserted into the narrow pockets) match painted wood frames. Contrast banding is a traditional trim for Roman shades.

Shades

Among the most practical window treatments, shades can be just as decorative as they are hardworking. Options range from soft fabric styles to high-tech versions.

With almost any shade, you can choose an inside or outside mount. A shade mounted inside fits neatly within the window opening, making it ideal for windows with handsome frames. An outside-mounted shade is attached above the window, on the frame or wall, and covers the frame or extends beyond at the sides and bottom when lowered. It's the preferred mount if you want maximum light control and insulation, or if you want to stack the treatment completely off the glass.

When is a shade the best choice?

■ When your window doesn't allow for full, fabric-rich treatments. Corner windows or closely spaced windows are candidates for simple shades, such as inside-mounted roller or cellular models.

■ When you want a crisp, clean look. A contemporary room calls for uncluttered window treatments, such as pleated or Roman shades. Roman styles include traditional (flat when lowered), soft-fold (forming loops of fabric when lowered), swagged (with tails at the sides), and stitched (often with dowels that keep the folds straight and crisp).

■ When you prefer a natural look. Woven shades bring subtle texture to windows.

■ When you want a fabric treatment, but one that doesn't extend to the floor. Tailored balloon and gathered cloud shades add softness to a room yet almost always stop at the sill or apron (the lower portion of the window frame).

■ When you want to use a minimum of fabric. If the fabric you've chosen is expensive, a flat shade such as a Roman or stagecoach style is a good option.

■ When your fabric features prominent motifs or a large repeat (the lengthwise distance from one motif to the next identical one). Gathered or pleated, such a pattern can look fragmented; shown flat on a shade, the design is clearly seen.

A woven shade with a self-valance is a handsome treatment for a casement window. Mounting the shade just below crown molding lengthens the look.

Visual Effects

Are your windows too narrow? Too wide? Do you wish they were set a bit higher in the wall? Designers use a variety of visual tricks to change the apparent size and proportions of windows. You can, too, with a little planning.

The mount, as much as the treatment itself, affects the appearance of a window. Inside-mounted shades and blinds emphasize the actual size of a window (below), or can even make

Inside-mounted roller shade

the window seem smaller—as is the case with sash or café curtains. You may like this effect on a small window in a cozy room.

Mounted outside, most coverings visually lengthen and widen a window (top center). To create an illusion of height, mount the treatment at the ceiling, just below crown molding, or partway between the ceiling (if there's no crown molding) and the window opening. A valance, cornice, or swag

Outside-mounted cornice and drapery panels

treatment installed above a window so that the lower edge just covers the top of the glass also lengthens the look. Floor-length panels elongate a window, although puddled panels may make a window appear shorter.

To shorten a tall window, hang a top treatment with its upper edge just above the frame (below), so that the

Outside-mounted swagged Roman shade

treatment extends well into the glass.

Curtain or drapery panels that almost clear the glass when fully opened can widen a narrow window (below). In the same way, you can make a wide window, such as a picture window, appear narrower by leaving some of the stack-back on the glass. With either approach, it's difficult to tell where the window starts and stops.

Cornices and valances emphasize the horizontal lines of a treatment and can subtly widen and shorten a window. Top treatments with shaped

Outside-mounted curtain panels

lower edges, such as a scalloped cornice, lessen this effect.

Where you place tiebacks or holdbacks on curtain or drapery panels is another consideration. When panels are tied or held back high, a window appears narrower; low tiebacks create an illusion of width.

Blinds

At first glance, blinds appear to be strictly functional. But they can play an important decorating role in both traditional and contemporary schemes. Slat width and material are the defining features.

Horizontal blinds. Made of metal or vinyl, horizontal blinds come in a wide array of finishes and colors. In metal blinds, you'll find three popular slat sizes. Micro-miniblinds, with 1/2- or 5/8-inch slats, are suited to small windows and windows with shallow sills. Standard 1-inch miniblinds are appropriate for most windows and decorating styles. Venetian blinds, with 2-inch slats and optional cloth tapes, can have either a contemporary or a retro feel. Vinyl blinds typically come in a range of sizes.

Wood blinds mimic the look of shutters at much lower cost. Painted, stained, and decorative finishes are available. For an understated look, choose a stain that's compatible with your walls, for example, a bleached or light pine stain in a creamy white room, golden oak or cherry in a room with richly colored walls. Wood blinds of all kinds can be purchased with cloth tapes, either plain or patterned. Slat sizes range from 1 to 3 inches.

Painted wood blinds make a natty undertreatment for a tab valance on a fabric-covered pole. Mounted outside the window frame, the blinds are concealed when raised.

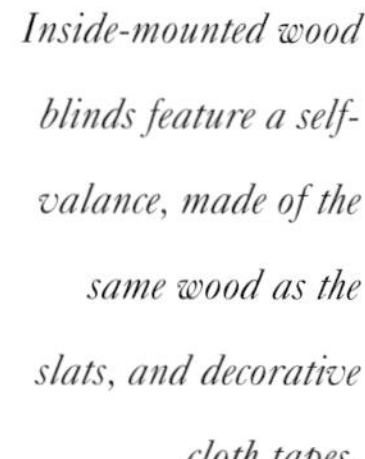

Inside-mounted wood blinds feature a self-valance, made of the same wood as the slats, and decorative cloth tapes.

Vertical blinds. Chosen more for their practical features than design attributes, vertical blinds are by nature contemporary. They come in a variety of textures and materials, most often fabric and vinyl. Vertical blinds may be attached to or encased in sheers (see page 105) if you prefer a softer look.

Both horizontal and vertical blinds are fine on their own, especially in minimalist schemes, and many styles have optional self-valances (made of the slat material) that cover the headrail. Often, however, blinds reside under top treatments such as cornices, fabric valances, and swags. Choose a top treatment in keeping with the style of the room—a gathered valance in a young girl's room, for example, or an upholstered cornice in a formal dining room.

Shutters and shoji screens

In a class by themselves, shutters contribute drama and architectural interest to both traditional and contemporary schemes. Consider your choices carefully; shutters are a big investment, and you'll want to be happy with them for a long time.

Once available only in wood, shutters now come in vinyl as well. The options in vinyl shutters are limited. Solid wood shutters, on the other hand, offer lots of frame styles, louver widths, colors, and finishes.

Traditional shutters. With 1¼-inch louvers, these shutters are suited to small- and medium-size windows and traditional decorating schemes. Narrow louvers cut down on the light entering the window and block the view more than wider ones, but they provide maximum privacy.

Plantation shutters. Wide-louver shutters allow better ventilation and a clearer view than narrow-louver styles. Types with 2½- and 3½-inch louvers are most popular.

An architectural element in their own right, plantation shutters let the sun stream in or tilt for privacy. Fold them back for an unobstructed view.

Shoji screens are traditionally used as doors and dividers, as well as window screens. Translucent inserts made of fiberglass diffuse light while ensuring privacy.

Innovative shutters. New to the window-treatment scene, these shutters feature materials such as translucent glass, acrylic (mimicking the rice paper of shoji screens), reed, and rattan suspended in wood frames.

Plan to blend shutters with either your walls or, more typically, your window frames for a unified appearance. Play with ways to fold the panels for different looks—open with a slight gap at the center, open but not folded back, or folded back all the way.

Shoji screens. A staple in traditional Japanese homes, shoji screens bathe a room in translucent light. Used over sliding glass doors and windows, shojis either glide in a track or, if hinged, fold back like shutters. The design lines of a shoji screen can affect the apparent proportions of a room: shojis with strong horizontal grids visually widen the window and enlarge the space, while vertical patterns can create an illusion of height.

Soft-fold Roman shades were the inspiration for tailored valances with contrast bands and covered buttons. Adequate wall space in the corner accommodates the folds of fabric.

Balloon valances with contrast pleats carry out a blue-and-yellow color scheme in a girl's room. Pleated shades hide underneath.

Valances

Once limited to staid, matching top treatments for curtains or draperies, today's valances are among the most imaginative and versatile of window treatments. They are typically paired with no-nonsense pleated or cellular shades or blinds, combining the softness of fabric with the practicality of a hardworking undertreatment.

Many valances are simply shortened versions of curtains, draperies, or fabric shades. Standard valance length is 12 to 18 inches at the center; shaped valances are longer on the sides.

- Rod-pocket valances are still a classic top treatment for curtain or drapery panels; arched, tapered, and scalloped valances are variations. Contrast banding or piping often punctuates the lower edges of rod-pocket valances.
- A wide-rod valance is simply a fabric sleeve for a rod up to 4½ inches wide; it may or may not have a ruffle above and below.
- Box- or kick-pleated valances make tailored top treatments. Box-pleated versions have equally spaced inverted pleats across the valance, with one pleat positioned at each corner. A treatment with a single pleat at the center and at each corner is called a kick-pleated valance. A Kingston (or bell) valance is a softer, more rounded interpretation of a pleated treatment.
- Balloon and cloud shades in shorter versions are ideally suited to valances. With either of these styles, the poufs or scallops along the lower edge are permanent, and the valance is stationary.
- Swags (mounted on a board or a pole) and scarves (draped through sconces) are considered valances when they top other treatments. Typically, the lower edge of the swag or scarf covers the headrail of the undertreatment.
- Stagecoach valances, shortened versions of the shades, can hang from a rod or be mounted on a board.
- Handkerchief valances, also called pennant valances, consist of flat panels with pointed lower edges. They often combine several colors and fabrics and may be edged with contrast banding and trimmed with tassels.
- Self-valances, stitched into the heading of a curtain panel rather than hung above the window, look much like a traditional valance when the panels are closed yet leave more of the glass uncovered when the curtains are open.

Cornices and lambrequins

Used alone or atop other window coverings, cornices and lambrequins are like blank canvases, waiting to be painted, stained, decorated, or upholstered.

Cornices. These structured top treatments serve two practical purposes: they block drafts coming from the window, and they neatly hide the heading and hardware of any undertreatment. They're a natural partner for blinds and shades, which can look unfinished alone.

Mimicking the look of deep crown molding, wood cornices come painted or stained. You can customize some wood cornices with decorative paint finishes. Others are constructed to accommodate standard-width wallpaper borders.

Upholstered cornices give a room a softer look. If your fabric has a noteworthy pattern, a cornice is the ideal treatment for displaying it. You can run the fabric vertically (a necessity if it has a lengthwise design) or horizontally (when there is no direction to the pattern). Running the fabric horizontally, with the selvage parallel to the lower edge, is most economical.

The lower edge of an upholstered cornice may be straight, arched, scalloped, or pointed. Optional embellishments include contrast or same-fabric piping, gimp, braid, and fringe, with piping the most popular trim.

A straight-edge cornice is a traditional top treatment for traversing draperies on a sliding door. Mounted just to cover the top of the frame, the cornice neatly hides the drapery heading.

Plan your cornice carefully; once it's ordered or constructed, you can't change it, even a little. The standard clearance on a ready-made cornice is adequate if it's going over a treatment that fits close to the window, such as inside-mounted blinds. For a cornice over an outside-mounted treatment, such as traversing draperies, calculate the clearance carefully.

Lambrequins. Elaborate cornices with "legs" that extend partway down the sides of the window or all the way to the floor, lambrequins are both decorative and functional. Because a lambrequin covers a greater area of the window, it's even more efficient than a cornice at keeping heat in and cold out in winter.

An upholstered cornice, gently scalloped along the lower edge, is an ideal top treatment for displaying a boldly patterned fabric. A woven shade underneath is both handsome and practical.

Silk cutout swags with full-length side panels soften tall windows but do not obscure their beauty.

A black-and-white scarf swag dresses a kitchen window. A casual rosette and jabot trim the treatment at the center; scarf holders support the fabric and form the tails.

Swags and cascades

These top treatments once graced the windows of only the stateliest homes, but today's versions adapt to both formal and informal decorating schemes. Swags fall into two categories: traditional and scarf.

Traditional swags. Although they appear to spill easily over a board or a pole, traditional swags are in fact highly structured window treatments, each made from a square or rectangle of fabric that's pleated or gathered on the bias. Swags may be solid semicircles of fabric mounted on a board, or they may be open at the upper edge and attached to a pole, forming a "cutout" swag. Use one traditional swag on a window up to 48 inches wide; for a wider window, plan to have swags overlap or just touch. Designers suggest that you use an odd number of swags so that one is centered on the window.

Cascades are gathered or pleated panels that hang at the sides of traditional swags. As a rule of thumb, cascades are at least twice as long as the longest point of the swag.

Shortened versions of cascades, jabots accent swags where they meet.

Most medium and lightweight fabrics that drape well are suitable for traditional swags; avoid stiff fabrics, such as glazed chintz or tapestry, that won't form soft folds. Because the lining shows on cascades, they provide the perfect opportunity to introduce contrasting color and pattern at the window. Accentuate the lines of the treatment with piping or fringe.

Scarf swags. These casual cousins of traditional swags consist of one length of fabric draped in sconces or other swag holders (see page 108) or wrapped loosely around a pole. If you decide to make your own scarf swag from a fabric other than a sheer, self-line the treatment so the wrong side doesn't show, or line it with a contrasting fabric as an accent.

Unusual windows

What if your windows are out of the ordinary? The solutions are varied—and often surprisingly simple.

Dormer windows. These charming windows are nestled into sloping roofs and are typically small, with little space on each side. How much space and how the window operates (most are double-hung or casement) dictate your window-treatment options. In general, stick to uncluttered treatments that require little or no stacking space. Lace or sheer rod-pocket curtains on a tension rod are traditional. For a more tailored look on a window that swings inward, mount a pleated or cellular shade (held down by brackets) on the frame itself; on an outward-swinging window, mount the shade above.

Clerestory windows. Also known as ribbon windows, clerestory windows run along the top of a wall near the ceiling. They're effective at admitting light and warmth into a room without sacrificing privacy, and for this reason, they are often left bare. If you must cover clerestory windows, keep the treatment simple —pleated shades, cellular shades, or blinds that stack up compactly, for example. Automated hardware or telescoping poles operate hard-to-reach treatments.

Geometric windows. When you must cover a geometric window for light control or privacy, choose a treatment that doesn't detract from the window's beauty. Pleated shades, cellular shades, and blinds can be custom cut to fit odd-shaped windows. For an understated look, match the treatment to the window frame or to the wall.

Skylights. These windows let natural light stream in, bringing warmth deep into a room without loss of privacy. But when there's too much light, glare, or heat gain, skylights require window treatments. Pleated shades, cellular shades, and blinds on tracks can be motorized or operated by a telescoping pole.

Hopper windows. The opposite of awning windows, hopper windows pivot at the bottom and open inward. Choose a treatment that clears the glass completely when the window is open. Shades or blinds mounted above the frame are practical. Sash curtains attached to the frame allow easy opening and closing of the window.

Roman shades on guide wires open and close over skylights, allowing full sun or filtered light.

Small windows placed high in the wall require no treatment other than painted frames.

design decisions

CHOOSING A *window treatment sounds easy enough—until you're faced with your own bare windows. Then all sorts of questions come up. As you approach the decision-making process, take a moment to consider the basics of color and design.*

A pencil-pleated cloud shade (above) made in a traditional floral print is sweet and romantic. Swags and cascades with full-length side panels and tassel fringe (right) are suited to formal schemes.

Getting started

You might begin by asking yourself a few questions about your decorating goals.

■ *What's your style?*
Decorating styles, many with exotic and romantic names, fill the pages of home magazines, but for the sake of simplicity, most can be described as either traditional or contemporary. The same is true of window treatments—most can be considered either traditional or contemporary, depending on the interpretation. Swags and cascades, for example, are traditional when they are structured and board-mounted, but casual when wrapped loosely around a pole or draped in scarf holders. Fabric also sets the style: patterned sheers say "contemporary," while their plain, pinch-pleated counterparts serve as modest undertreatments in traditional homes.

Hard window treatments such as miniblinds and pleated shades are generally considered contemporary, yet they work in traditional schemes as well, especially when teamed with traditional top treatments. Shutters and wood blinds adapt to either style; the material, louver width, and finish determine the effect.

To help you select a treatment, turn to the gallery of ideas (pages 34–79) and see what looks appropriate for your windows and your home. The more you analyze decorating styles, the easier it is to make good choices.

■ *What role will your window treatments play?*
Do you envision elaborate swags that take center stage—or plain curtains that barely get noticed? In general, the simpler the treatment and the fabric, the less you will be aware of the windows. Unless yours are noteworthy, stick to treatments that support the room scheme, rather than command attention, and consider your options in the context of other materials in the room. Whenever possible, buy a yard of a fabric you like, attach it to the wall or window, and step back to see its visual impact.

Unstructured swags with short cascades and long bows top stationary side panels in a mint-green garden room. When window treatments blend with or match the wall color, the effect is harmonious.

Window treatments that contrast with the walls, such as these ruffled cloud valances, stand out. Be sure to vary the values (lights and darks) of other furnishings and accessories to balance the scheme.

■ *What's the scale of your windows and room?* Scale is one aspect that's easily overlooked when formulating a window-treatment plan. The conventional wisdom is that smaller-scale treatments—shutters with narrow louvers, curtains on slender rods, and flat valances—are best suited to small windows and small rooms. Larger windows and rooms are thought to be the best place for large-scale treatments—plantation shutters, curtains on bold rods, and billowy valances. Although it's a good idea to take into account the scale of your home, also think about the look you hope to achieve. Simple curtains on small hardware will recede in a large room, while bold treatments will advance in a smaller space. Peruse decorating magazines, and you'll see examples of treatments that defy the conventional wisdom, to great effect.

■ *What's your preference—blended or contrasting treatments?* This question is an important one, because how much a window treatment contrasts with the walls dramatically affects a room's ambience. A treatment similar in value (see page 22) to the walls—pale blue cloud shades against creamy white walls, for example—will quietly blend into the room and put the focus elsewhere.

Another way to blend window treatments with walls is to repeat the wall or trim color—patterned yellow curtains against yellow walls, for example, or ivory-colored Roman shades mounted inside ivory-trimmed double-hung windows. Hard window treatments are often chosen to blend with the walls or trim.

High-contrast window treatments attract more attention and are more difficult to pull off. The treatment may be much lighter or darker in value than the walls, or the colors may come from opposite sides of the color ring (see page 22). Contrasting window treatments will stand out in a room, but keep in mind that your attention may stop at the window. If the view is outstanding, opt for a blending—rather than a contrasting—treatment.

For help in choosing colors, patterns, and textures, see pages 22–25.

A monochromatic scheme works best when you vary the values of the chosen hue, such as the pale green walls and darker green smocked curtains in this sitting room.

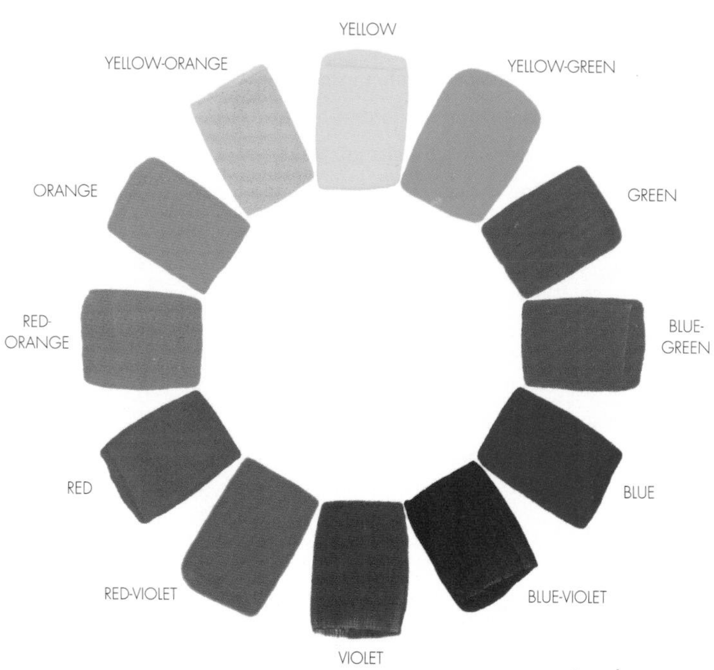

Color basics

If you think you're not good with color, take heart: a familiarity with some simple color terms and concepts can help you achieve the look you want with window treatments.

Color characteristics. Window materials offer a wonderful opportunity to pull together a decorating scheme with color. Three key color characteristics—value, temperature, and intensity—determine the impact of a window treatment as much as color itself. If you can learn to recognize and work with these characteristics, you can combine almost any colors in a room.

Value is the lightness or darkness of a color. Robin's-egg blue is a light value, and navy blue is a dark value. In between lie medium-value colors, such as chambray blue. When a window treatment is similar in value to the walls—pale curtains in a room with pale walls, for example—the effect is quiet and harmonious. If a treatment contrasts sharply in value, however—dark pleated shades in a white room—the treatment may dominate the room, an effect you may or may not like.

Visual temperature has to do with how warm or cool a color feels. Greens, blues, and violets are considered cool, while yellows, reds, and oranges feel warm. For a unified effect, choose window treatments whose visual temperature is similar to that of the walls, such as warm pink-and-yellow balloon shades in a yellow room. The same balloon shades in a minty green room will seem more prominent.

Intensity is the brightness or dullness of a color. Apple green is an intense version of yellow-green, while sage is a low-intensity version of the same yellow-green. Almost without exception, your attention will go to an intense color before a low-intensity one. Who pays attention to olive drab—and who can avoid staring at chartreuse? Choosing window treatments that are similar in intensity to the wall color and furnishings is one way to unify a room.

Color combinations. You don't need to know color theory to put together a smashing color scheme, but an acquaintance with the color ring shown on the facing page can get you started. There are three basic kinds of color combination— neutral, related, and contrasting.

Neutral combinations consist of black, white, gray, and very low-intensity colors such as taupe and camel. Neutrals are favored for window treatments in subdued schemes, especially when the walls are also neutral.

Related schemes are made up of variations of one color (called a *monochromatic* scheme) or colors that lie side by side on the color ring (called an *analogous* scheme). If you plan to use just one color, be sure to use slightly different values and intensities of that color, such as a range of light-to-medium, dull-to-somewhat-brighter versions of peach. Otherwise, a one-color scheme can be monotonous.

For an analogous scheme, such as blue, blue-violet, and violet, consider adding accents of a color opposite on the color ring (yellow-orange, a color you might call "papaya," in this example) to balance the visual temperature.

Contrasting color schemes are surprisingly simple to implement. Colors that lie directly opposite on the color ring are known as *complements*. Red and green are complements; so are violet and yellow. Three colors equally spaced on the color ring make up a *triad*. There are other classic color combinations, but in general, if colors are balanced or equally spaced on the color ring, the scheme will be pleasing.

Whether you're working with "givens" or starting from scratch, look to the color ring to help you build a harmonious scheme. If your carpet is a low-intensity green, for example, consider terra-cotta, approximately opposite green on the color ring, for window treatments and, in a lighter version, for walls.

You can also take your color cues from a favorite fabric—many multicolored fabrics are examples of beautifully balanced color combinations. But don't try to match other materials, such as flooring or wall color, to your lead fabric. A little dissonance is more appealing.

Whatever your color scheme, repeat the colors throughout the room. A window treatment whose color doesn't relate to any other element in a room will stand out—or worse yet, look like a mistake.

Blue and apple green (yellow-green) are not side-by-side on the color ring but are still considered analogous colors. In a two-color scheme, use a mix of patterns, as in this Roman shade.

Complementary combinations can be surprisingly soft. Low-intensity red and olive green (a version of yellow-green), near complements on the color ring, are compatible because they are muted.

Pattern and texture

Patterned or plain? Smooth or nubby? When to use patterned or textured materials in window treatments is an important decision because both qualities affect our perception of color. A few terms and guidelines can help you combine patterns and textures with confidence.

Pattern scale. The relative size of the motifs or designs in a pattern is known as scale. Scale is usually described by designers as small, medium, or large.

Small-scale patterns in window treatments tend to read as textured or solid from a distance. Use them with solids or as visual relief among other patterns.

Medium-scale patterns are versatile because they maintain their design, even from a distance, yet rarely overpower other patterns. Most patterns are medium in scale.

Large-scale patterns may look fragmented if pleated or gathered; be sure to scrunch up or fold a potential fabric before you commit to it.

One-color schemes like the one below lend themselves to bold patterns. Don't attempt to match the colors in patterned materials—slight differences add interest.

Floral and striped patterns on windows and walls combine easily when they share similar or related colors.

Pattern panache. You'll have the most success with pattern if you follow this advice from designers: choose patterns that are different enough to be interesting yet similar enough to be harmonious. Here's how.

- Combine various patterns. Naturalistic patterns, such as florals, mingle easily with stripes and plaids.
- Use a mix of pattern scales—but don't vary them too much. To a medium-scale floral, for example, you might add a smaller-scale plaid. A large-scale pattern and a miniprint may look incompatible.
- Create places for the eye to rest in the room by introducing solid or textured materials.
- Distribute pattern throughout a room; if you cluster patterns, the room may look lopsided.
- Unite different patterns with a common characteristic, such as color. A floral, stripe, and plaid can be pleasing together if each contains a similar—but not necessarily matching—color, such as several versions of pink.

Pattern possibilities. Because window treatments and walls touch in a room, it's impor-

Window treatments have both actual texture, which you can feel, and visual texture, which you perceive. A mix of both kinds of texture is most effective, especially in a neutral color scheme.

tant to consider the options for patterned and plain color. Following are the most common ways to treat windows and walls.

- Plain walls and plain window treatments are harmonious and easy to pull off. You see this approach often in monochromatic (one-color) schemes. Vary the textures for added visual interest.
- Plain walls and patterned window treatments are popular in both traditional and contemporary schemes. Choose a window-treatment fabric or material that repeats or echoes the wall color, such as a soft blue-and-yellow stripe in a room with pale yellow walls.
- Patterned walls and patterned window treatments work best when one pattern dominates, such as subtly patterned walls and more strongly patterned window treatments. If you use the same pattern at the windows and on the walls, choose one you'll love to live with. Used throughout a room, any pattern will appear bolder.
- Patterned walls and plain window treatments work when the colors are similar in intensity, such as low-intensity celadon (gray-green) balloon shades juxtaposed with subdued pink-and-green wallpaper.

Texture tips. All fabrics possess texture, from obvious to exquisitely subtle. Hard window treatments, such as woven-wood shades, are also textured; even miniblinds have a "texture," which is smooth. Texture is important because it influences and modulates color in powerful ways. On shiny surfaces, a color appears lighter; on textured surfaces, the same color appears darker. Yellow silk curtains, for example, will look lighter than crushed-velvet panels in the same yellow.

Combining textures, like mixing patterns, is a balancing act. Here are a few simple guidelines.

- Use a variety of textures in a decorating scheme, just as you would patterns. In a room with a leather sofa, rattan chair, and handwoven rug, cotton duck panels are pleasing.
- If your color scheme is neutral or monochromatic (see page 23), use lots of different textures, especially if there is little pattern among your materials.
- Unite a room by using similar textures. In a dining room with gleaming wood floors, treat the windows to shimmering silk curtains. In a family room with a twill sofa, choose Roman shades of nubby linen.

Light streaming through a split-bamboo shade casts a pattern on gingham curtain panels. Wood beads visually tie together the two treatments.

practical matters

WINDOW TREATMENTS *do much more than just adorn windows. For just a moment, set aside questions of style and focus on practicality.*

Functional considerations

Does light stream through your windows, overheating your home? Do you need more privacy? Can you childproof window treatments? To best meet your needs, consider the myriad functions of window treatments.

Gauzy linen panels hanging from square rods and rings are meant to blow in the breeze when the French doors are open. In an indoor/outdoor room, minimal treatments strengthen the visual link between interior and exterior spaces.

LIGHT CONTROL. Allowing natural light into a room is one of the primary functions of windows, and "lots of light" is usually on everyone's wish list for a home. How much light enters depends on the number of windows; their size, shape, and orientation; buildings or plants outdoors; and the window treatments.

If your goal is to admit maximum light, choose treatments that clear the glass when opened or raised. Draperies (with adequate stack-back on each side) or outside-mounted blinds (with adequate stacking space above) are two options. To filter light and control glare, consider sheer panels, horizontal or vertical blinds, translucent pleated or cellular shades, woven shades, or shoji screens.

The most effective light-controlling treatments are outside-mounted curtains, draperies, or fabric shades that are lined, especially those with blackout linings. Blinds of all kinds, when tilted, block most of the light. Some pleated and cellular shades feature two fabrics, one opaque and the other translucent, for maximum flexibility in light control.

CLIMATE CONTROL. There's nothing like a breeze through an open window to cool your home. For the best ventilation, choose window treatments that stack back or up completely; stationary panels or deep valances that cover part of the glass will block the flow of air.

You can't consider windows and climate control without taking into account energy efficiency (see page 106).

PRIVACY. In the daytime, it's difficult to see into a house because the interior is usually darker than the outdoors. Sheer and translucent treatments of all kinds provide some daytime privacy while allowing light to enter.

But at night, when homes are lit, it's easy to see through uncovered windows or windows with translucent treatments. To ensure nighttime privacy, choose a treatment that

A sheer Roman shade allows privacy and filters light during the day; pleated curtains on rings close easily at night.

provides maximum coverage, such as lined curtains, draperies, or fabric shades that close or lower completely. Most of the hard window treatments, such as cellular shades, wood blinds, and shutters, also provide excellent nighttime privacy. If you don't like the look of blinds or shades on their own, hide them during the day under a top treatment.

VIEW. When the view deserves to be seen, choose a treatment that clears the glass completely; windows with lovely vistas are not the best place for panels tied back low or top treatments that cover much of the glass. A treatment that blends with the walls focuses attention on the outdoors, rather than the window.

If the view is unattractive, choose a white or light-colored treatment that admits light when lowered or closed—and keep it that way. Shutters with narrow louvers and micro-miniblinds are both effective at blocking the view, even to some extent when tilted open.

SAFETY. If you have young children or pets, window-treatment safety is a primary concern. Following are some of the safety features you'll find in today's products.

■ Cordless horizontal blinds and cellular shades are available; ask your dealer for product information. With a cordless mechanism, you simply grasp the middle of the bottom rail and lift or pull down.

■ On two-cord shades, cut the cords above the tassel; then add a separate tassel to the end of each cord. Most high-quality blinds and shades come with breakaway tassels, which separate under pressure.

■ For continuous-loop systems, most common on vertical blinds and draperies, install a permanent tie-down device or cleat to the wall or window frame.

■ Replace looped cords with a wand.

Measuring Windows

To estimate the cost of most window treatments, you'll need to measure your windows. If you order window treatments from a mail-order source, look for detailed instructions in the catalog. For accuracy, use a steel tape measure.

For a treatment mounted inside the window, you need only measure the width of the opening (A) and the length (B). Measure at the top, middle, and bottom of the frame; use the smallest measurement.

For outside-mounted treatments, also measure the area to be covered to the left (C) and right (D) of the opening, called the extensions, and the distance above the opening (E). This distance is typically 4 inches for curtains, draperies, and valances, but it can be less if you want to mount the hardware just above the window frame or on the frame itself.

The distance below the opening (F) varies, depending on the treatment style. Apron-length treatments usually end 4 inches below the opening. Floor-length treatments generally end $1/4$ to 1 inch from the floor; allow extra length for puddled panels.

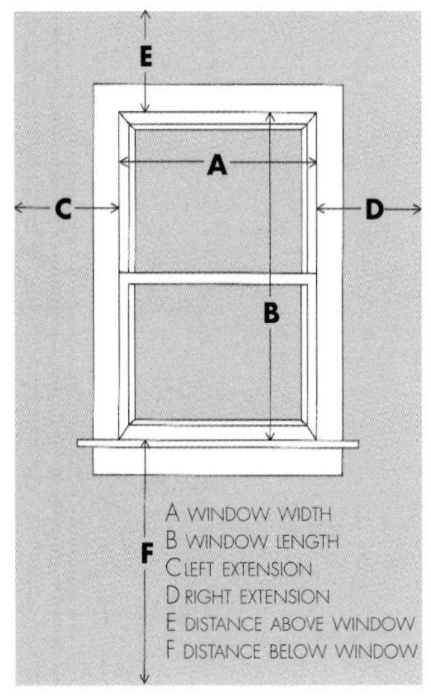

a window-treatment sketchbook

"**What am I going to do** *with these windows?" Whether you're envisioning bare windows in a new home or puzzling over what to do with existing windows, window-treatment decisions do not always come easily. Rather than focusing on the coverings, why not start with your windows? Windows are, after all, the reason for window treatments, and the more thought you give to their attributes (and limitations), the happier you'll be with your choices. Determining which treatments work best on which windows is what this section is about. On the following pages, you'll find 11 window styles, each handled two different ways. Take a look.*

Arched

The arched, or Palladian, window has a long, illustrious history. Semicircular windows, called sunbursts, flourished in the 1700s, and elliptical fanlights appeared later, in the American neoclassical revival. Today's "postmodern" arched windows, popular in new construction, can be integral or have double-hung or casement windows below the fanlight.

Because the arched window is such a noteworthy architectural element, many homeowners choose to leave it untreated if privacy and light control are not issues. Or, leave the arch exposed and treat only the area below with curtains, draperies, shades, or blinds.

Fan-shaped pleated and cellular shades that cover just the arch are available; plan to use a matching shade to cover the rest of the window. Shades and blinds can also be custom-cut to fit an arch, with the slats running horizontally. You can't raise the treatment, of course, but the slats will tilt. Custom wood shutters that cover the entire window are handsome but expensive.

Arched
Goblet-pleated panels

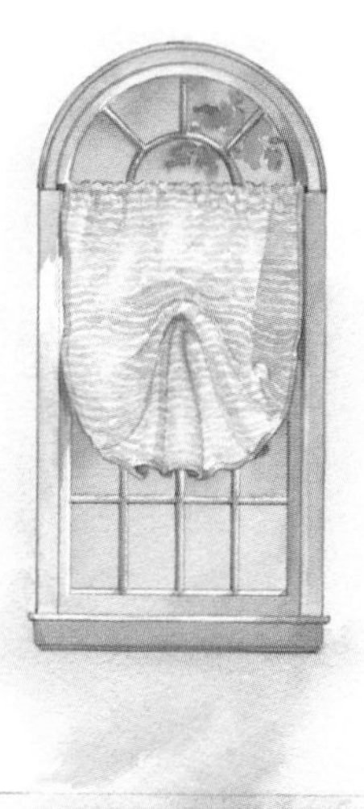

Arched
Sheer London shade

Most fabric treatments that follow the curve of the arch, such as curtains on a custom-bent rod, draperies attached to a wood frame, or simple swags, are stationary and purely decorative.

Awning

Like casement windows (see page 30), awning windows are hinged and swing outward. But they're hinged at the top, not on the side, and they're usually rectangular.

Awning windows come in a number of configurations, all of which provide good ventilation. They typically occur in combination with fixed-glass windows, with the awning portion at the top or bottom of the unit.

Awning
Wood cornice and woven shade

Roman, roller, pleated, or cellular shades, along with horizontal blinds, are good choices if your awning window is at the bottom of a fixed unit because you can raise the treatment just enough to allow ventilation, yet keep the upper portion of the window covered for sun control. Avoid treatments that tie back low, such as stationary curtains; they may interfere with the handles. Curtains, draperies, and vertical blinds that stack off the window are other practical options.

Awning
Roman shade

An awning window at the top of a fixed window is a good candidate for a top-down/bottom-up shade, allowing you to bare the awning portion while maintaining privacy below.

Bay and Bow

Graceful and romantic, bays and bows are windows everyone loves to have in a home—but few know how to treat. A bay is a recessed window with angled sections; when the sections are set in a gentle curve, the window is called a bow. If the view is outstanding and privacy and light control are not concerns, this is a wonderful window to leave uncovered.

Bay
Rod-pocket curtains

Most bays and bows, however, require window treatments. If your bay features handsome window frames, consider playing them up with individual, inside-mounted café curtains, shades, or blinds. Roman shades with contrast banding are tailored and traditional.

Over simple shades or blinds on closely spaced windows, add a continuous valance or a series of shallow swags. Plan carefully so the top treatment conceals the undertreatments when they're raised.

Rod-pocket curtains and curtains on rings require a hinged, flexible, or custom-bent rod. If there is space, hang a stationary panel between windows and at each outer window. For a bay or bow with little space between windows, flank the entire window area with a pair of panels and top the treatment with a cornice.

Bay
Swags, cascades, and café curtains

Casement

Hung singly or, more typically, in pairs, casement windows have sashes that are hinged on the side and crank or push outward. In a pair, only one window may be operable while the other is stationary, or both may open. Casement windows often flank fixed-glass windows.

Casement
Tab curtains

Window treatments that clear the glass completely when stacked back, such as curtains on rings or draperies, flatter the vertical lines of a pair of casement windows and allow maximum light and ventilation. Blinds and shades of all kinds are also appropriate. To soften the look of hard treatments, add a simple valance or a wood cornice.

Traditional swags and cascades are suited to the graceful proportions of casement windows. A scarf swag wrapped around a decorative pole is a casual alternative.

Casement
Woven shades

If you prefer to cover some of the window—perhaps the view is not altogether desirable—consider gathered or pleated curtains that meet in the center and tie back low. On a pair of windows where only one operates, hang a single curtain panel and tie or hold it to the fixed side of the window.

Cathedral

Typically angled at the top to follow the slope of the roof, cathedral windows are among the most difficult to treat. If they happen to be placed high, with no possibility of outsiders seeing in, the angled portion is often left bare. Besides, untreated windows allow the most light and reveal the best view.

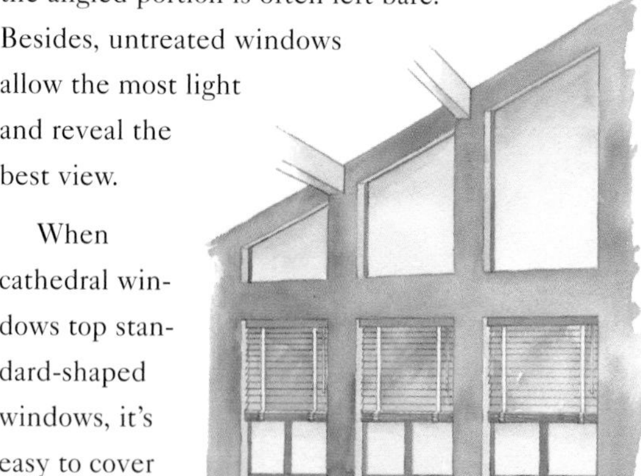

Cathedral (uncovered)
Wood blinds (below)

When cathedral windows top standard-shaped windows, it's easy to cover the lower windows with miniblinds, wood blinds, pleated shades, woven-wood shades, cellular shades, or vertical blinds. Simple curtains on rings and traversing draperies (space permitting) are suitable if you prefer a soft fabric treatment. Because this window is contemporary, stick with a simple window covering and avoid voluminous fabric treatments, such as swags or balloon shades.

Cathedral
Cellular shades

Because sun control and heat gain can be major problems with cathedral windows, homeowners often cover the entire window area with individual treatments, such as horizontal blinds, custom-pleated shades, or cellular shades. Although the manufacturers don't recommend raising the shades beyond the point where the angle begins, many homeowners do just that by pulling one of the cords. Be aware, however, that you'll have uneven cords hanging down after the shade is raised.

Corner

The two types of corner window are those that meet glass to glass, at a right angle, and those that are separated by window frames or wall space. Choose a treatment based on the way your windows meet and the amount of space, if any, between them. In general, avoid fabric treatments with fullness in the corner, which can make the area look cluttered.

Corner
Swags and cascades

Curtains on rings, one-way draperies, or vertical blinds that open from the corner are ideal for a glass-to-glass corner window, whose primary attribute is an unobstructed view. Just be sure the window treatment stacks back completely when opened; otherwise, the window will appear smaller.

Corner
Scarf swags with miniblinds

If your corner windows are separated by wall space or window frames, almost any inside-mounted shade or horizontal blind will work—for example, roller shades, pleated shades, woven-wood shades, or wood blinds. Avoid outside-mounted versions unless there is adequate room; when raised, the treatments may collide in the corner.

Top treatments unify corner windows. A continuous valance or scarf swag that turns the corner teams nicely with blinds or shades.

Double-hung
Pleated panels

Double-hung

These are windows everyone likes, as much for their graceful proportions as their hardworking features. Double-hung windows have two sashes—an upper, outside sash that moves down and a lower, inside sash that moves up. Used alone, in pairs, or in groups, double-hung windows allow for almost any window treatment.

Casual curtain options include tab, rod-pocket, and flat or pleated panels on rings. Traversing draperies, topped with a shaped valance or cornice, are dressier. With a curtain or drapery treatment, decide whether you want the panels to stack back completely, revealing the window frame, or to partially cover the glass.

All of the tailored shades suit double-hung windows—Roman, pleated, cellular, and woven-wood. Most shades can be inside- or outside-mounted; with cloud or balloon shades, choose an outside mount to accommodate the volume of fabric.

Traditional swags and cascades are a time-honored treatment for this classic window; scarves are less formal and show off more of the frame.

Double-hung
Swagged shade

Picture

Used alone or in combination with sliding or casement windows, picture windows (also called fixed-glass windows) let in plenty of light and frame the view. Because of the size and shape of picture windows, however, finding the right treatment can be a challenge; choose one in keeping with the proportions of the window.

When operable windows flank a fixed window, it's important to select a treatment that stacks back completely. Full-length curtains, draperies, or vertical blinds allow good ventilation when fully opened, and their stack-back helps balance the large window area. On a window without operable side windows, you can leave some of the stack-back on the glass if the view is less than outstanding or if you want to create the illusion of a narrower window.

Fixed glass
Flat panels

Consider top treatments for picture windows carefully. A deep valance can accentuate the window's width; a gently scalloped valance or a shaped cornice that just skims the top of the glass can soften the lines and create the illusion of a slightly taller window.

If you opt for blinds, pleated shades, or cellular shades, check with the manufacturer to make sure the treatment comes in the width you need. For very wide windows, plan to mount multiple treatments on a single headrail.

Fixed glass
Scalloped valance and panels

French Doors

Elegant and graceful, French doors are at the top of the list of desirable windows. They usually consist of a pair of matching glass-paneled doors, one or both of which open. With outward-swinging French doors, almost any treatment is appropriate. On doors that open inward, however, the treatment must clear the door frame or be attached to the doors themselves.

Sash and hourglass curtains made of lace or sheers were once the standard treatment for French doors. Blinds are a more up-to-date option, but keep in mind that they will move with the doors; attach clips at the bottom to hold the treatment in place. Avoid heavy fabric shades, such as soft-fold Roman shades.

Formal French-door treatments include draperies that stack completely, topped by a matching valance or cornice. Pleated curtains on rings can be formal or casual, depending on the fabric and the hardware. Swags and cascades require adequate space above so that the lower edge of the treatment doesn't dip into the doors.

French doors
Crinkly sheers

French doors often have transoms (windows above) or sidelights (vertical windows flanking the doors). You can treat the entire area as one or cover each section separately.

French doors with transom
Scalloped valance and panels

Sliders

Composed of two or more panels, sliding glass windows and doors are among the most utilitarian of windows. Easy operation should be a primary consideration when you're choosing a treatment for a sliding door.

SLIDING DOORS
VERTICAL BLINDS

Draperies on one-way traverse rods allow for convenient opening of sliding doors but require a large stacking area; you may decide to keep some of the stack-back on the fixed portion of the door. Vertical blinds stack back compactly, making them a good choice where space is tight. Like draperies, they have the added benefit of allowing passage without uncovering all of the glass. Another option is a vertical pleated or cellular shade.

If you opt for horizontal blinds, pleated shades, or cellular shades for a sliding door, choose a style that stacks up compactly. It's best to mount two blinds or shades on one headrail, permitting you to raise just the one over the operable part of the door.

On sliding windows, top any of the hard treatments with a shaped valance or simple cornice. Pennant valances, with their irregular points, break up the strong horizontal lines of sliding windows. Shutters on sliders add architectural interest to a room.

SLIDING WINDOWS
PENNANT VALANCE

Tall Windows

Windows of grand proportions lend themselves to equally elegant treatments and trimmings in a formal scheme. If the room is large, consider voluminous fabric treatments, such as goblet-pleated draperies or traditional swags and cascades. Even a treatment as simple as rod-pocket curtains looks luxurious on a tall window if the fabric is sumptuous silk.

TALL WINDOWS
SWAG VALANCE AND PANELS

Tall windows are ideally suited to top treatments over traversing or stationary panels. An upholstered cornice with a shaped lower edge, used in combination with draperies, constitutes a formal, traditional treatment. Arched or scalloped valances, sometimes too fussy for windows of lesser proportions, are graceful in combination with curtains. One advantage of tall windows is that a top treatment may extend well into the glass area and the effect will still be pleasing. For sun control and privacy, add sheer draperies or a woven shade.

TALL WINDOWS
GATHERED VALANCE, PANELS, AND CLOUD SHADE

In starker settings, tall windows can accommodate contemporary treatments, such as sheer curtain panels or pleated shades. Choose blending—rather than contrasting—treatments to minimize the window's proportions. Use a telescoping pole to operate a hard treatment, or automate it.

NANTUCKET ISLAND

GREAT WINDOW TREATMENTS

IT'S TIME TO GET INSPIRED! And as you'll quickly discover in this photo-filled chapter, ideas for great window treatments are both plentiful and varied, sometimes to the point of pleasant confusion. YOU CAN APPROACH your search for a suitable window treatment in one of several ways: You might look carefully at the examples of a particular style, such as a cloud valance or curtains on rings. Does the treatment seem appropriate for your windows? Is it practical for your life-style? Will it fit in with the style of your home? Or simply peruse the pages and see what strikes your fancy among this collection of window fashions. Perhaps you like the softness of lace panels, the elegance of silk swags, or the simplicity of pleated shades. THE IDEAS ARE HERE; take them all in and consider them carefully. The perfect window treatment for your windows and your home may be one you're about to see.

curtain call

These casual curtains appear to fold forward at the top, but each "valance" is actually a separate piece of fabric stitched to the top of the panel. (To achieve a similar effect without piecing, you must line each panel with the same fabric.) Contrast banding emphasizes the edges.

Pleats tacked at the top of the heading fan out for a relaxed look. These unlined linen panels, like the other treatments on these pages, are technically curtains because they are sewn to wood rings and are moved by hand.

A layered treatment in an attic hideaway consists of semisheer and sheer panels, both pleated and attached to small rings.

Pleated curtains are relaxed yet crisp, thanks to crinoline (a stiffener) stitched into the heading of each panel. Curtains that match the window trim blend into the room for a quiet effect.

sheer simplicity

An ivory lace valance, drawn up at the center and each corner, bears a slight resemblance to a swagged Roman shade; a smaller, one-scallop version is just right for a tiny corner window. Mocha-colored trim unites the window treatments and walls.

Lace panels with pointelle edging hang from tension rods. Flat, rather than gathered, curtains are ideal for showing off delicate patterns.

A lace curtain tied to one side covers a plain sheer in an elegant white-and-silver powder room. Subtle patterns and textures, at the window and on the walls, play an important role in a minimal color scheme.

SPRUDEL

Rod-pocket sheers are scooped back by the arms of a wicker love seat. A woven shade underneath is both practical and decorative.

Fan-pleated sheers feature a wide band of brown silk near the lower edge; a narrow band placed high repeats the color and accentuates the lines of the clerestory window.

Gauzy tab curtains create the perfect backdrop in a dramatic dining room. Short, wide tabs hang from metal poles with birdcage finials.

Loosely woven linen panels, casually pleated at the heading, hang softly from wood pegs. The upper-edge trim and graceful bows are sewn from an iridescent, copper-colored semisheer. Both fabrics marry well with decorative paint finishes and architectural elements throughout the room.

THE GREAT MASTERS

A length of fabric, "swagged" and attached to a custom-cut board, follows the elegant curve of a wide arched window. (This treatment is sometimes referred to as a "portiere drapery.") Patterned sheers diffuse light.

Striped sheers crisscross at the top of arched windows, then puddle gracefully on the floor. Metal holdbacks gather the panels to each side.

Contemporary sheers, slit in a fashion reminiscent of cutwork embroidery, reveal the exquisite lines of French doors and an arched transom.

versatile shades

Copper mesh Roman shades with brass grommets and exposed cords filter light and create horizontal bands of color as they are raised.

Fringed Roman shades mounted below elliptical windows are a slight departure from tradition. Trim of any kind can visually unify window treatments and other elements in a room.

Striped Roman shades keep their crisp pleats by means of narrow dowels slipped into stitched pockets. Repeating the wall color in the window treatments unifies the room and highlights French doors and sidelights.

Stitched Roman shades, with the tiny tucks toward the window, are a classic treatment for tailored schemes. Mounting the shades above the window opening lengthens the look.

An unlined linen shade filters light and softens a pair of casement windows in a cloakroom; inverted pleats, embellished with sisal buttons, are the only details. A scalloped wood valance complements the simple shade.

Mounted at the soffit of a bay, swagged shades visually elongate a trio of windows. A single pleat on both sides of each shade helps shape the scallops.

Plain and simple, a burlap shade adds neutral color and nubby texture to a pantry window.

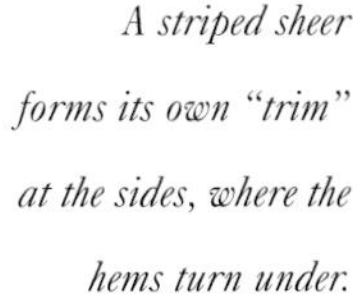

A striped sheer forms its own "trim" at the sides, where the hems turn under.

Natural shades in a window seat control sun when lowered yet do not block the view. Woven shades work well in a scheme that includes other patterns and textures.

Outside-mounted woven shades with self-valances visually unify different, yet closely spaced, corner windows.

An antique Japanese shade rolls forward, held up by cording attached to bronze hooks. Silk brocade binds the edges; black tassels embellish the treatment.

billowy clouds

The same floral fabric looks different gathered into cloud shades than it does spread across the bed. Gingham ruffles in compatible colors trim the shades and the bolster.

Silk celadon shades dress a recessed window and nearby windows in quiet, elegant color. Thick welt, knotted at the ends, finishes the upper edges. Pink-and-green tassel fringe links the window treatments to walls and furnishings.

A blue-and-white cloud valance, shirred at the heading and ruffled at the lower edge, is a romantic top treatment for a little girl's room. Miniblinds underneath control light and maintain privacy.

shutters and shojis

Shoji screens offer the best of both worlds: when closed, they bathe a room in translucent light, yet they still provide daytime privacy. These screens glide in tracks for easy opening and closing.

More than just a window treatment, traditional shutters are an important architectural feature in a room. In this tailored scheme, stained wood shutters unify large and small windows.

Custom-painted plantation shutters display their own color scheme, echoed in the room's furnishings. Painting the frames, slats, and tilt bars different colors emphasizes their structure.

Reeded-glass panels diffuse and distort light for privacy during the day. They are appropriate in both contemporary and traditional schemes.

top treatments

Tab-top valances with short, shallow box pleats and pennant points team with plantation shutters in a bay. Tassels punctuate the lower edges.

A bright cloud valance on a wide rod sports a contrasting rod pocket and ruffle; narrow gold welt and puffy stars trim the treatment.

Matching fabric ties hold up an outside-mounted stagecoach valance. (Notice that the pattern aligns on the ties and the face of the shade.) Stained wood blinds with cloth tapes echo colors in the botanical fabric.

Tall windows and high ceilings accommodate fabrics with large-scale patterns, such as this multicolored cornucopia print. (Careful centering of motifs is a must with large-scale patterns.) Woven shades underneath the balloon valances and on the door do the real work.

A balloon valance made of crinkly silk frames the view in a stunning bow window. Sumptuous fabrics and trims turn simple styles into elaborate treatments.

Pleated bells add classic detailing to a tapered Kingston valance (also called a bell valance). The lower edge just skims the top of the window, allowing the most light and the best view.

Cascades and stationary side panels turn a tapered Kingston valance into an elaborate, formal treatment. Italian tapestry trims the edges.

This "green room" is dressed in a Kingston valance and lacy shades, all trimmed in green gingham. Individual shades are ideal in a bay; the continuous valance ties together the treatment.

Gently gathered and scalloped silk valances top matching side panels in a grand dining room. Mounting the top treatments just below the crown molding allows the handsome—and different—transom windows to show. Woven shades make practical undertreatments.

A box-pleated valance, ever so slightly gathered, and matching side panels cover a pair of casement windows. The spacing of the embroidered motifs determined the size of the pleats.

Kohler & Campbell

An upholstered cornice doubles as a shelf and a top treatment for a banded Roman shade. Textured, tone-on-tone fabrics add visual interest to a neutral scheme.

A shaped cornice finished with self-welt follows the line of a noteworthy transom window. Matching Roman shades mounted on French doors control light and ensure privacy.

A marbleized wood cornice with gold highlights is the focal point of this sleek curtain treatment. The rod-pocket panels are made of antique satin, trimmed with a contrast fabric and tied back with cord and tassels.

Casually gathered, these traditional swags and cascades are nevertheless formal. A small center swag balances the outer ones in the starring treatment; stationary side panels are held back low. Single swags are in scale with smaller windows.

A "country" fabric goes formal when made into traditional cutout swags. The treatment appears to be continuous, but it's just an illusion—each swag is constructed and attached separately. Stationary side panels frame the window.

A straight cornice edged with welt provides the backdrop for a series of overlapping swags. Because the French doors open inward, the entire top treatment must clear the frame. Stationary side panels feature bishop's sleeves.

pattern play

A blue-and-yellow toile pattern has a different look on walls, windows, and beds. Swagged valances trimmed in tassel fringe team with sheer white shades with slats that tilt like blinds.

Dressing the walls, windows, and bed in the same quiet fabric is a recipe for tranquility. Stripes accentuate the graceful lines of traditional swags and cascades. Shutters are appropriate companions for soft fabric treatments.

Nearly identical patterns (one is checked, the other not) adorn the windows and walls in a bedroom hideaway. Fan-pleated curtains on rings are trimmed with tassel fringe and tied back low.

yellow is primary

Gathered "pleats" give curtains on rings their fullness and shape. Gingham welt and lining complement the floral pattern; a Roman shade is a practical and decorative undertreatment.

Cloud shades made of silk taffeta contrast quietly with green walls and white trim in a formal sitting room. Lace sheers dress the French doors.

Bright, bold scalloped valances, mounted just below the crown molding, are paired with matching side panels in a sunny bedroom. Tassel fringe repeats the color scheme; plaid lining peeks out from under the valances and leading edges.

TURN A SPECIALTY WINDOW INTO A COZY HIDEAWAY

window seats

Shallow single pleats accommodate the bulk of embroidered and interlined cotton panels in a window-seat bay.

A pencil-pleated valance and pleated side panels make up a simple treatment for a wide window seat. Miniblinds underneath allow room darkening.

A contemporary window seat gets treated to a fresh cloud shade. (The narrow ruffle is cut from the blue-green stripe in the fabric.) Companion fabrics and a wallpaper border complete the look.

Stitched Roman shades dress a window seat in crisp blue and white. A medley of patterns gives this two-color scheme variety.

special effects

Tab curtains take on a whole new look when the fabrics are luxurious silks and velvet. Chenille caterpillar fringe trims the side and lower edges; a chenille rosette decorates the base of each tab.

Voluminous, one-of-a-kind silk swags frame outward-swinging French doors. The color scheme is analogous (page 23), ranging from peach through pink, with values (page 22) that vary from light to medium. French wire ribbon is the only embellishment.

An unlined silk curtain ties to one side for a look that is nonchalant but elegant.

Stripes and a curvilinear design are pleasing in combination when they share colors and textures. Silk welt separates the banding from the panel.

Pinch-pleated panels make the most of a striped silk fabric. By spacing the pleats so that they fall only in the ivory stripes, the taupe sections dominate the heading. As the panels open toward the bottom, the stripes are revealed.

A simple treatment, rod-pocket curtains, goes formal when the windows are beautifully proportioned and the fabric is silk. The panels are interlined for body; they hang from oversize gold- and silver-leaf rods.

not just for windows

Sheer bed curtains (below) consist of flat linen panels hanging from tiny colored rings. Details make a difference (bottom), no matter how simple the treatment or the hardware.

A box-pleated valance and stationary panels look just as appropriate dressing a bed as a window. Companion fabrics unify the treatment.

Satin ribbons threaded through grommets and tied into bows (above) are a variation on tabs. Ceramic holdback (left) made of tile shards and offbeat embellishments dresses up the plain panels.

FLOWERS
YOUR
FOR
ARE SWEET

A SHOPPER'S GUIDE

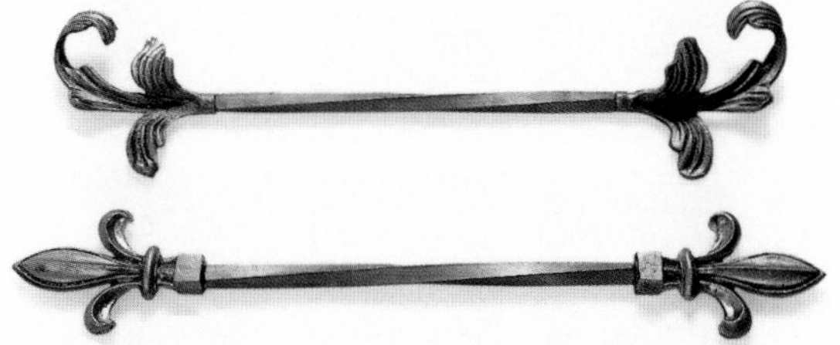

WHETHER YOU START OUT with a few notions about the best way to handle your windows or glean some concepts from this book, you still must put those ideas into action. If you're set on shades or shutters, what are your choices? If blinds are the ticket, what are the various styles you're likely to find? How do you choose curtain or drapery fabric? What's new in decorative hardware? **THIS CHAPTER** will help you find the perfect off-the-shelf solution or custom window treatment. You'll discover what's available in the marketplace, where to shop, and what features to look for. You'll also find practical tips on installing and caring for window treatments. There's even advice on new windows, in case ugly or rickety ones are inhibiting your choice of window coverings. **THE WORLD** of window treatments awaits you—and it's full of more products and possibilities than ever before.

Windows

THE FRAME FOR YOUR DISPLAY

There are good reasons to consider your windows themselves when you're making decisions about window treatments. After all, the new treatments will draw attention to the openings on which they are placed.

Are your windows suitable companions for the coverings you favor? Perhaps your interior decor—including your taste in window coverings—is traditional or country, while your aluminum sliders typify the 1950s ranch-style house. Or maybe you'd like luxurious, high-quality coverings but don't want to waste them on unattractive or dilapidated windows.

If your inclination is to disguise problem windows, you may end up with different coverings—and a completely different look—than you desire. Hiding such windows may conflict with your need to keep them uncovered for at least part of the day, to maximize sunlight, let in fresh air, or enjoy a view. Should you conclude that your windows need replacing, you can console yourself with the fact that good-looking, well-built, energy-efficient windows are an investment that adds to a property's value. Plus, they help show off beautiful window treatments.

Choosing windows

The range of windows available today is staggering. Manufacturers produce literally thousands of standard variations, from arched casements, old-fashioned bays, and fixed windows in semicircles, ovals, trapezoids, and other shapes to hinged or sliding French doors, all with an assortment of framing and glazing options, many designed for energy efficiency. If the window you want isn't standard, most manufacturers will make one to your specifications. As an alternative, you can group standard windows in unusual configurations to achieve a unique custom look.

Windows are sold through many sources, including manufacturers, name-brand dealer networks, window stores, home centers, and building-supply yards. Often, the window you order is built at the factory and then shipped to the dealer, where it's prepared for installation before being delivered to you. If you prefer, you can probably find a company that manufactures windows closer to home; there's less risk of damage to the product in transit, and you can work with a local supplier.

A good-quality window should be solidly constructed with strong, tight joints and smooth operation. Sashes should open easily and close flush all around, and window locks should shut securely without undue force. Each pane should be fully sealed in the sash, and weather stripping should provide a continuous seal around the window.

FRAMES. The most common window-frame materials are wood, clad wood (the wood is covered with a thin layer of vinyl or aluminum), vinyl, and fiberglass (a relative newcomer). A less familiar option is steel. Neither steel nor aluminum frames are nearly as insulating as the other types. Of the more energy-efficient frames, clad wood and fiberglass tend to be costlier than wood or all-vinyl. Wood units require regular refinishing and can rot if not properly maintained. Vinyl frames require the least maintenance; clad wood and fiberglass demand little upkeep if you don't paint their factory finishes.

Glazing. Many of the greatest strides in window technology are taking place in glazing. Most quality windows sold to homeowners today include insulating glass, which is made of two or more panes of glass sealed together, with a space between panes to trap air. Low-e (low-emissivity) glass usually consists of two sealed panes separated by an air space and a transparent coating to reflect heat and screen out the sun's ultraviolet rays. Some window manufacturers use argon gas between panes of low-e glass to add extra insulation.

Warm-edge technology is another feature offered. Instead of an aluminum spacer between panes of insulating glass, warm-edge windows have a less conductive spacer that won't transfer heat as easily. The result is less condensation buildup around the edge of the window, often a problem in cold climates.

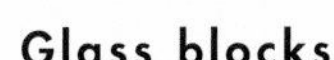

Glass blocks

Where privacy is important but opening the window isn't, you may opt for a glass-block window instead of a standard one. Often used in bathrooms, where moisture can be ventilated with a fan, glass blocks let in soft, diffused light. The blocks themselves become the window treatment.

You can buy 3- or 4-inch-thick glass blocks in many sizes; rectangular and curved corner blocks are also available in a more limited selection. Textures can be smooth, wavy, rippled, bubbly, or crosshatched. Most block is clear, though Italian block also comes in blue, rose, and green tones, and German block in a gold tone.

Glass blocks are usually sold individually and are mortared together on the job. Prefabricated panels are sometimes available, but they're very heavy. Installation of any type of glass block is best left to a professional.

To locate glass block, look in the yellow pages under Glass—Block. You may be able to special-order blocks through a regular glass or tile dealer.

Glass blocks

Fabric

LET'S GET MATERIALISTIC

To anyone browsing through bolts of fabric or stacks of swatches, it's obvious that fabrics come in an astonishing range of choices, many of them suitable for any given window treatment. Some basic facts about fabric and a few shopping tips will help you select with confidence.

Understanding fabric

Fabric is a material made up of a fiber, such as cotton or rayon, or a blend of fibers. (For details on the most common fibers, see the chart on page 87.) But shopping for fabric isn't as simple as asking to see a cotton or rayon curtain material. That's because the same fiber can be made into diverse fabrics; for example, cotton can be woven into filmy scrim, crisp chintz, plush velvet, lustrous damask, or stiff canvas.

Usually, the heavier the fabric, the tighter the weave should be if the treatment is to hang properly. The looser the weave, the more a fabric is affected by heat and moisture. In humid climates, the hemline in loosely woven draperies can rise and drop noticeably.

A pattern can be woven into or printed onto a fabric. In woven patterns, which are durable and generally costly, the colors show in a reverse design on the wrong side. In printed patterns, dye is applied to the surface, though it often seeps through to form blurry images on the opposite side. Modern fabric mills use machinery that can print dozens of colors, making more intricately hued, richer fabrics possible. For example, you can buy affordable printed versions of such expensive woven fabrics as damask.

Although some fabrics hold their colors better than others, an absolutely colorfast material doesn't exist. Bright colors appear to fade more than subdued colors, and solids more than prints. Sun rot can be another problem. If the window treatment will be exposed to strong sunlight, choose a rot-resistant fiber such as linen, polyester, or acetate.

Choosing fabric

An interior designer can show you material suitable for your situation. But if you're shopping on your own and fabric stores are unfamiliar territory,

Fabric stores often group patterned fabrics by dominant colors.

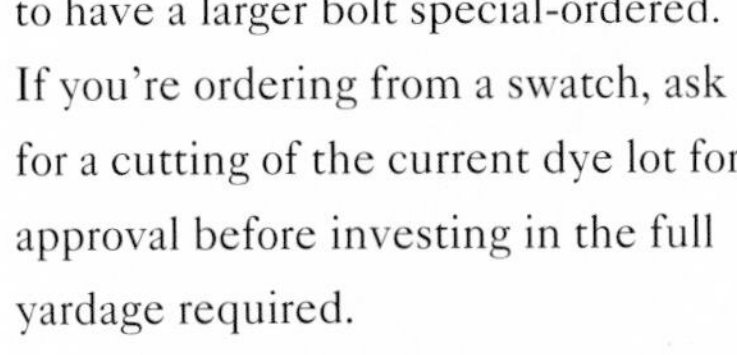

here are some guidelines. You'll be looking at the store's decorator fabrics, which are often grouped apart from garment fabrics.

Most decorator fabrics are 54 inches wide and are wound on cardboard tubes rather than flat cardboard. They usually have a higher thread count (they're more tightly woven) and stand up better over time than garment fabrics. Because they're not preshrunk, they shouldn't be washed. Another reason to avoid laundering them is that they're treated with finishes to make them resistant to stains, mildew, and wrinkles and to add more sheen or stability.

Consider a fabric's suitability for the window treatment you're planning—for instance, fabric for a swag should be supple, and one that will be drawn up in folds should have body without being too heavy or stiff. Check on fiber content and special finishes, information usually printed on the selvage (finished edge) or on the label. When choosing more than one fabric for a single window treatment, such as a curtain panel with contrast banding, look for similar weights and cleaning compatibility.

A knowledgeable salesperson can help you choose, as well as figure out how much fabric to buy. Take along paint chips, carpet scraps, and upholstery samples from the room that will contain the new window covering. Also bring accurate measurements of the window (see page 27 for measuring instructions) and your plans for its treatment.

Don't just look at a serious contender on the bolt. Unroll several yards and gather one end in your hand. Does it drape well? Does a pattern hold its own, without getting lost in the folds? Stand back several feet to see how it looks from afar. Ask for samples so you can examine them at home in daylight and under artificial light. If a sample is too small, consider buying ¼ yard.

Once you've decided on a fabric, buy all you need at one time—and, if possible, from one bolt. Before cutting, though, unfurl the bolt and inspect the fabric for flaws. Slight color differences among bolts may be noticeable in the finished window treatment. If not enough fabric is available on a bolt, ask to have a larger bolt special-ordered. If you're ordering from a swatch, ask for a cutting of the current dye lot for approval before investing in the full yardage required.

Choices, Choices

Many fabrics are suitable for window treatments. If you're overwhelmed by the possibilities, check out these tried-and-true choices.

- Plain, patterned, or crinkled sheers for diaphanous curtain or drapery panels
- Semisheers, such as lightweight linen or lace panels, for a bit more privacy
- Chintz, a type of polished cotton print, for curtains, draperies, fabric shades, or valances
- Cotton/linen prints, including tea-dyed or old-world look-alikes, for all types of treatments
- Toile, which depicts country scenes in one color on a light background, for a variety of treatments
- Soft, drapable sateen, antique satin, or shantung for swags or draperies
- Lightweight velvet for curtains or draperies
- Cotton duck or ticking for Roman shades or tab curtains
- Canvas for simple panels and flat valances
- Jacquards—heavy tone-on-tone fabrics including damask, brocade, and tapestry—for formal draperies and cornices

Comparing costs

Fabrics sold through interior designers usually cost the most. Retail outlets that rely on sample books generally sell at higher prices than stores that stock fabrics by the bolt.

You can save money by buying "seconds"—fabrics that have minor defects, though sometimes they're simply overruns. Some outlets sell seconds clearly marked as such; others mix seconds with first-quality fabrics and offer them at the same price. If you see flaws on a fabric and it's not marked as a second, ask about it.

When comparing the cost of two fabrics that look the same, make sure they really are the same. Fabric houses often "down-print" a pattern on a less expensive or flimsier fabric—one that may not hold up as well as you wish.

Sheers come plain, patterned, or crinkled and in classic white or colors.

What next?

If you've chosen material on your own and don't sew, who will fabricate the window treatment that you have in mind? A designer or decorating service may agree to work with your fabric—or you can go directly to a drapery workroom, the place where designers go to have window coverings made for their clients.

Some workrooms will just fabricate the treatment you want based on measurements you give them; others offer a turnkey operation including measuring, fabric selection, and installation.

Because selling fabric is a source of profit for most workrooms, they may charge an extra fee for using fabric you've purchased elsewhere.

To find a drapery workroom, look in the yellow pages under Draperies, or ask at a fabric store. Get references and check them; also find out if the workroom guarantees its work in writing.

Comparing Fibers

NATURAL FIBERS

Cotton

Advantages. Stable and durable; myriad weights, textures, and patterns.

Disadvantages. Fades and rots in direct sun; mildews; shrinks with washing; burns unless treated.

Linen

Advantages. Strong and durable; resists sun rot.

Disadvantages. Fades in direct sun; wrinkles unless blended with a more stable fiber, such as cotton or polyester; can stretch or shrink in humid climates unless blended with a nonabsorbent synthetic fiber, most commonly polyester; burns unless treated.

Silk

Advantages. Long-lasting if lined and kept out of direct sun; versatile (can be made into fabrics as different as chiffon and velvet).

Disadvantages. Fades and rots in direct sun; wrinkles; mildews; shrinks with washing or in humid climates; picks up static electricity; burns unless treated.

Wool

Advantages. Durable; more stable if blended with a synthetic fiber.

Disadvantages. Fades and rots in direct sun; reacts to humidity and temperature changes; picks up static electricity; burns unless treated.

SYNTHETIC FIBERS

Acetate

Advantages. Stable; colorfast when solution-dyed; resists sun rot; melts rather than burns.

Disadvantages. Wrinkles; picks up static electricity.

Nylon

Advantages. Stable and durable; washable; wrinkleproof; melts rather than burns.

Disadvantages: Fades and rots in direct sun; picks up static electricity; has a synthetic appearance unless blended with other fibers.

Polyester

Advantages. Stable and durable; colorfast and resistant to sun rot; washable; wrinkleproof; often made into fabrics that look like silk; blends well with other fibers.

Disadvantages. Picks up static electricity.

Rayon

Advantages. Drapes well; dyes well, making it available in beautiful, sophisticated colors; blends well with other fibers.

Disadvantages. Rots in direct sun; mildews; shrinks when washed; wrinkles unless blended with a more stable fabric; burns unless treated.

Linings: The Inside Story

A lining acts as a buffer between the decorative face fabric and the sun, the window glass, and any dust or dirt drifting in. It improves the way the window covering hangs and gives the window a finished look from outdoors.

With swags, cascades, and other treatments where the lining shows from the front, line with the same or a coordinating fabric. Where the lining is hidden, use a special fabric sold as "lining."

Some linings resist water stains or ultraviolet rays. Others are designed for energy conservation. Still others completely block light.

Most window-treatment linings are made of cotton or a cotton-polyester blend. They're usually sateen, a strong, tightly woven fabric. Insulating and blackout linings are laminated with vinyl or layered with foam acrylic.

White, off-white, and ecru are the standard colors sold; fade-resistant colored linings are also available. Interlining is a soft, loosely woven fabric used between the lining and the face fabric to provide extra insulation and body. Soft cotton flannel is a common choice, as is "bump," an English felt.

Trims

FABULOUS FINISHING TOUCHES

Trims are an easy and clever way to give an ordinary window treatment a custom look or fancy finish. They are useful in accenting a window treatment and in emphasizing its shape and form. The embellishments range from thick, corded tiebacks and tasseled fringes to ruffled lace trim and velvet ribbons. These trimmings are known collectively as *passementerie*.

Tassels are sold by the piece, other trims by the yard. Look for a wide assortment in fabric stores and shops specializing in drapery and upholstery supplies, or order them through an interior designer. Of the items described here, tassels are commonly found in mail-order catalogs and retail stores that sell decorative window hardware and ready-made curtain and drapery panels. You can also make your own tassels from kits.

High-quality trimmings from a decorator or designer showroom are beautifully constructed (sometimes by hand), luxurious-looking, and expensive—you can easily pay hundreds of dollars for a single tassel. Trims from retail sources, including fabric and drapery supply stores, aren't as lavish, but the cost is much less.

Trims are available in natural or synthetic fibers. High-end items are often made of silk, linen, cotton, or wool, with rayon or viscose sometimes added for sheen. Many mass-marketed products are made of polyester, rayon, or acetate. Popular chenille trims are made from various fibers. Some of the more exclusive or innovative trims incorporate materials such as crystals or wood or ceramic beads. Additionally, some manufacturers offer metallic jewelry ornaments in various motifs, such as butterflies or dragonflies, that you can pin onto window treatments.

Choose trimmings that are compatible with the weight of the fabric or other material used

Tassel fringe and jumbo tassels on tiebacks are color-coordinated with multihued silk curtains.

in the window treatment. Also consider care and cleaning of trims that will be attached permanently. Use washable trims (and prewash them) on curtains or other window treatments that will be laundered, and dry-cleanable ones on treatments that will be sent to the dry cleaners. When shopping for trims, bring along a sample of the window-treatment material so you can see how the colors and textures blend. And take home a piece of the trim to see how it looks in the room.

Here are definitions of some trims commonly used as flourishes on window treatments.

Braid. A flat border, usually 1 to 3 inches wide, with two finished edges.

Cord. A rope made up of twisted strands or fibers, often used as a tieback for curtains or draperies. Lipped cord has a narrow flange that allows the cord to be sewn into a seam.

Eyelet. A flat or ruffled fabric trim with small holes. Eyelet beading has slits through which ribbon can be threaded.

Fringe. A border with short strands of yarn or cord on one edge. Types with densely packed, often multicolored cut threads are called brush fringe. Those with twisted strands are called rope fringe or bullion. In loop fringe, the strands are looped instead of hanging free. Other variations include caterpillar fringe (tubed yarn), ball fringe (little balls), tassel fringe (tassels), and tasseled bullion (a combination of yarn strands and tassels).

Gimp. A narrow braid, up to about ½ inch wide, with looped or scalloped borders.

Tassel. A dangling ornament made by binding strands of yarn or cord at one end. The most common type is a tassel tieback, which consists of one or two tassels attached to a looped cord or rope and is used for holding back curtains or draperies. Specialty trims include the swag tassel, which is designed to be suspended from a top treatment.

Welt. A fabric-covered cord, available in various diameters from about ¼ to 1 inch, with a narrow flange that can be stitched into a seam.

The various types of fringe, cord, and braid shown here can add flair to draperies, soft fabric shades, swags, and other window coverings.

Hardware

A NEW ACCENT ON STYLE

Until recently, most of the window-treatment hardware readily available to consumers was manufactured by just a few companies and consisted of a limited selection of rods, rings, and finials. For more interesting—and much costlier—hardware, you had to order through a decorator or find a shop specializing in brass or other metalwork.

Now choices abound, thanks to an explosion of interest in home decorating. You'll find all kinds of appealing, useful, and affordable items in fabric stores, linen and bedding shops, home furnishing stores, mass-merchandise outlets, and mail-order catalogs. Where you might once have seen a preponderance of strictly functional hardware that was meant to be concealed, today decorative items rule the racks.

The following are the main types of rods and accessories you'll encounter.

Stationary rods

These include decorative models for hand-pulled curtains attached by tabs, ties, rings, hooks, or clips, as well as concealed types for fixed panels, such as sash curtains, rod-pocket curtains, and valances.

Decorative rods. In the past, most of the widely sold metal rods were café models: narrow-diameter, round or fluted brass rods with understated finials. The café rods are still around, but in colorful painted finishes as well as brass. The metal-rod category has grown to include rods of assorted diameters and finishes, including bright or antiqued brass, wrought iron, verdigris, brushed nickel, and pewter.

These decorative metal curtain rods and finials of metal, glass, and ceramic are just a few of the scores of readily available hardware possibilities.

Some rods adjust to various lengths, while others come in fixed lengths to accommodate a number of window widths.

Rather than resting immobile in brackets, some decorative metal rods are hinged so you can swing the rod with its curtain away from the open window or door. You move the swing rod back toward the window when you want the glass covered.

Wooden poles are sold plain or fluted in a choice of diameters (typically 1⅜ and 2 inches) and various lengths (most commonly 4, 6, or 8 feet), which can be cut to fit. You can get poles unfinished, stained, or painted in solid colors as well as distressed, crackled, or otherwise "antiqued."

The many types of metal rods and wood poles are supported by brackets that you attach to the wall or window frame. If a rod is longer than about 5 feet, you'll need a center support, which is usually in a loop shape. Though some rods and poles incorporate finials, many accept screw-in finials of your choice. These end pieces can give your window treatment a lot of extra appeal. (See the section on Accessories on pages 92–93 for more about these items.)

Pole sets, which have a wood or metal finish but are actually constructed of rolled steel, usually come complete with pole, finials, and decorative brackets. The poles are adjustable in length.

Wire rods are newcomers to the decorative-rod category. The rod is sold with a length of wire, special brackets, and a center support. You attach the curtain (lightweight fabrics are recommended) to the wire with decorative clips.

Whimsical clips attach a lightweight curtain to a wire curtain rod.

Concealed rods. The most familiar type is the adjustable white metal lock-seam rod, though other, more stylish choices in various metallic finishes are available—and with those, you won't mind if some of the hardware is visible. With a standard lock-seam rod, you insert one piece into another, then snap the ends onto brackets that you affix to the wall or window frame. Single flat rods are made with projections (the distance they stick out from the bracket) ranging from about 1¼ to 6 inches. Those with deeper projections, allowing them to clear other treatments beneath them, are sometimes called valance rods. Double and triple rods accommodate layered treatments.

Other common concealed options are the sash rod, which holds sash or hourglass curtains neatly against French doors and casement windows, and the tension rod, which has a spring mechanism to keep the plastic- or rubber-tipped ends snugly within the window frame.

Yet another type is the wide-pocket rod, available in widths up to 4½ inches. Inserting the rod into a heading on an abbreviated panel is a quick, easy way to make a shirred valance. An optional foam fascia that snaps onto the rod can be covered with fabric for an instant cornice. Special corner brackets allow you to use wide-pocket rods in bay windows.

Other concealed rods include flat types hinged to fit corner and bay windows, and custom-bent and flexible rods to follow curves on arched windows. Purely functional swing rods are also available.

Traverse rods

These adjustable rods are used for draperies that open and close with a cord or a wand. The rod contains sliding holders, called carriers, into which you slip the drapery hooks. When the draperies are closed, the rod is hidden; when they are open, the rod is visible unless cloaked by a top treatment.

A two-way traverse rod, which moves the panels from the center to the ends and back, is standard. A one-way traverse rod, which moves only one panel in one direction, is used over sliding patio doors or where two windows meet at a corner. Custom traverse rods for bay or other odd-shaped windows can be special-ordered from drapery suppliers. On all types, you need a center support, which fits over the rod and screws into the wall, for rods wider than about $4\frac{1}{2}$ feet.

Decorative traverse rods work the same way as conventional types, but they're designed to be seen whether the treatment is open or closed. The draperies are attached to rings that slide on a concealed track. Many people prefer a decorative stationary rod and rings to which they attach curtain hooks or clips. The greater choices in stationary rods makes up for having to move the fabric panels by hand.

Accessories

The strictly functional accessories stocked by stores carrying curtain rods include items such as weights for drapery hems, extension plates for mounting brackets beyond the window frame without putting holes in the wall, and stackable shims to build out blind and

Decorative brackets and holdbacks come in many materials and winsome motifs. Some are meant to be attached to the tops of window frames, while others are designed to sit at the sides of windows.

shade brackets to clear window trim or handles. Various gizmos designed to help you create no-sew top treatments, such as plastic valance pleaters, are also sold.

Additionally, you'll find lots of useful but highly decorative items, including finials, ornamental brackets, holders for swags and scarves, and holdbacks. All offer many opportunities to be creative with window treatments.

Once plain and unadorned, rings, clips, and hooks now come in many stylish designs.

Finials. These end pieces add a lot of character and charm to a window treatment. You'll find an intriguing selection in a wide range of sizes, motifs, and finishes including various metals, wood, glass, ceramic, rattan, and molded resin. Finials come in innumerable shapes, including spears, arrows, balls, leaves, pineapples, moons, stars, suns, scrolls, birdcages, flowers, and seashells.

Brackets. Once strictly utilitarian or unimaginative in design, these supports, which you affix to the top outer edges of the window frame or to the wall, now come in an extensive array of motifs.

Types sold for supporting a rod or pole range from subtly decorative to highly ornate, and they come in the same materials as rods and finials. With some, you set the rod or pole in a depression in the bracket; others have a loop that you place the rod through. A center bracket, typically in a loop shape, is usually recommended for rods longer than 5 feet.

Many products labeled as "sconces" or "scarf holders" are ornate brackets with a hole in the middle (it is visible only from the side) that you can use to support a rod or thread a swag or scarf through—or you can use the same brackets to serve both functions. Generally quite large and sculptural, these brackets are often made of resin molded into shapes such as animal and human figures, grape clusters, flowers, and leaves.

Holdbacks. These include various types of decorative hardware for holding draperies and curtains, or even tailed swags and scarves, to the sides of a window. Some styles can be mounted at the tops of windows and used in the same way as brackets to anchor swags and scarves; others are inappropriate for that use.

Holdbacks come in various sizes, designs, and finishes, just as brackets do. Most consist of a plate that you attach to the wall or window frame, a stem that juts out several inches, and a decorative front piece. If the decorative piece is hooked, you tuck the fabric into the hook; otherwise, you secure it behind the front piece. You can also attach tassels and other tiebacks to this type of hardware.

Rings, clips, and hooks. These once-simple items for attaching curtains and draperies to rods have acquired some flair over the years. Today's options include wrought-iron rings in various finishes, sleekly twisted hooks, and clips hidden behind decorative faces shaped like leaves, stars, and other objects.

Ready-made Panels

QUICK MAKE-OVERS FROM THE SHELF

Buying stylish ready-to-hang panels is a good alternative to having curtains or draperies made to order, if you lack the desire or budget for a custom job. Or time may dictate an off-the-shelf purchase—perhaps overnight guests are due shortly and the windows in your spare room are still bare.

Look for ready-made curtain and drapery panels in retail outlets such as linen and bedding shops, home furnishers, department stores, and mail-order catalogs. In addition to stocking panels for standard windows, many suppliers carry panels for doors and sidelights (glass on either side of a door). Most also carry decorative rods and other hardware for hanging the panels, as well as matching valances, scarves, and other top treatments.

Appealing choices

You'll encounter styles ranging from casual to dressy. Some incorporate trimmings: you'll find panels embellished with lace, fringe, ruffles, and ribbons. Lengths range from short café curtains to long panels that are meant to puddle luxuriously on the floor. Drapery panels are generally pleated. Curtain panels, when mounted, may be tightly gathered, slightly gathered, rippled, or nearly flat; attachment options include rod-pocket sleeves and decorative loops, ties, bows, tabs, grommets, rings, and clips. You'll also find novelties, such as sheer panels with pockets at intervals along the surface for displaying small items (see opposite page, bottom right photo).

Among the many fabric choices are gauze, scrim, lace, ticking, toile, velvet, denim, canvas, sailcloth, and damask. Some fabrics consist entirely

The ready-made panels shown here and on the facing page demonstrate a few of the many style, fabric, and color possibilities. Tab tops, rod-pocket sleeves, and rings are common methods of attachment.

of a single fiber type (for example, cotton, polyester, or silk), while others are blends (for instance, jute and cotton creating a linen look). Most ready-made panels are unlined and require dry cleaning to prevent shrinkage and to preserve their look, feel, and finish.

Formerly available in a limited range of solid colors and prints, today's ready-made panels come in an enticing array of colors, plaids, florals, geometrics, and playful prints. Even sheers, once largely restricted to plain white and ecru, include colorful as well as patterned and crinkled choices.

Matching scarves are optional with some panels. They are often sold in a set width and in a choice of yardage, such as 4, 6, or 8 yards.

Select carefully

Before shopping, ascertain the dimensions of your windows (see page 27 for instructions on measuring) and any adjacent areas you want to cover. The total panel width you need depends on the type of panel you choose. With nearly flat panels, you'll need little more than the actual width you measured. With gathered panels, figure on getting twice the measured width. For door panels, add just a few inches. If you don't intend to close curtain panels but rather want them to frame the window, get a width adequate for your purpose. In most cases, you'll want just two panels for each window: divide the required width by 2 to find the ideal panel width.

Also consider how long the panels should be. For floor-length panels, figure on stopping from ¼ inch (many professionals use this figure for traditional draperies on traverse rods) to about 1 inch above the floor. Long curtain panels in soft fabrics can puddle on the floor. The length of shorter curtains depends on how far above the window frame you intend to hang them and how far below you want them to extend—some suppliers suggest 4 inches above and 4 inches below the window.

Ready-made panels may be sold individually or in pairs. The width is listed first, then the length. Most panels are available in a single width and several lengths, although some come in a choice of widths as well. Some curtain styles lend themselves to doubling up panels on each side for wide windows. If you're in doubt, consult the supplier.

Be sure to deal with a reputable company. Many firms will accept returns if you don't like the way the treatment looks when you hang it, but check on the return policy first. When dealing with a catalog company, be aware that colors may not reproduce faithfully; to be safe, request swatches before ordering the panels.

Installing Curtain and Drapery Rods

For a complicated or heavy window treatment, it's best to have professionals handle installation. But some setups are so simple that you can easily install them yourself.

Choosing a fastener

For a sturdy installation, use a fastener suited to the surface and strong enough to bear the hardware and the fabric. For the most secure attachment, plan to screw into the window casing or into wall studs.

Use wood screws (not the nails that come with some hardware), substituting longer screws for the ones that the manufacturer provides if they look inadequate or you feel extra strength is needed. When drilling into the window casing, positiion your drill bit at least 1/4 inch from the edge of the molding to avoid splitting the wood. If you're drilling into the wall around the window, you have a good chance of going into solid wood—the window is framed with doubled studs at either side and a header on top.

If you must attach brackets to plaster or wallboard, use plastic anchors or toggle bolts—but limit this to only the lightest treatments.

To fasten hardware to aluminum, vinyl, fiberglass, or steel window frames, use self-tapping or sheet-metal screws. On a brick or concrete surface, use masonry bolts with expanding plugs.

Each element in a layered window covering needs adequate clearance. Here, a valance rod with a deep return provides ample room for the traverse rod beneath to operate smoothly. Likewise, the traverse rod's return permits a comfortable gap between the back of the draperies and the front of the stationary curtain panel on the tension rod.

Installing the rod

The first order of business is to decide where the rod will go and to mark the brackets. Positioning conventional draperies on a traverse rod is easy if you imitate the professionals who leave 1/4 inch between the bottom of the draperies and the floor. Since a little fabric is taken up by the rod itself, you'll automatically achieve that spacing by setting the top of the brackets at a height equal to the finished length of the draperies.

With a decorative rod, placement depends on the curtains' method of attachment to the rod—for example, tab-top panels will hang lower than rod-pocket panels—and on the design of the brackets. Place the panel on the rod and have someone hold it up for you to see.

Once the rod is properly positioned, hold up the brackets in the appropriate locations and mark them with a pencil. Before drilling, use a carpenter's level to be sure the rod will be level. Don't just follow the lines of the window frame: if the frame isn't square, the rod will be crooked and the fabric won't hang properly.

Drill holes for the screws or bolts and fasten the brackets securely in place. For a heavy or wide panel, add support brackets every 4 or 5 feet to keep the rod from bowing. You can open adjustable rods to the maximum recommended length if you use an extra support.

Shades

TRADITIONAL TO HIGH-TECH LOOKS

There's no shortage of choices in window shades! They run the gamut from no-frills, ready-made vinyl roller shades that sell for only a few dollars to handwoven, motorized Roman shades costing thousands of dollars. Although traditional shades that draw up or roll up in tidy or billowing folds are still very popular, high-tech styles continue to make inroads. These newer shades include types with an insulating honeycomb design, and ones made of sheers with fabric slats between that tilt like horizontal blinds.

Function is important in choosing a shade. Consider whether the shade is suitable for the window type and size. Decide whether you want filtered sun, a clear view, privacy, or room darkening, then test the fabric (ask for swatches) to see if it serves your purpose. For energy conservation, pick a shade that covers the entire window surface snugly with no gaps. If you need a shade that's wider than standard for that particular product and the supplier suggests overlapping or seaming, ask to see a sample before you purchase.

A shade should be neatly finished, with no frayed edges. If the shade is unlined, consider how it will look from the street. Be sure the operating mechanism works smoothly: the shade should remain level when you raise and lower it, and it should stay where you stop it. Various mechanisms include standard cords, continuous or looped cords, beaded chains, and battery-operated remote controls. For a shade positioned over a stairwell or other hard-to-reach area, a telescoping pole will allow you to hook onto the cord or onto a ring attached to the end of the cord and pull; automated operation is a costlier alternative.

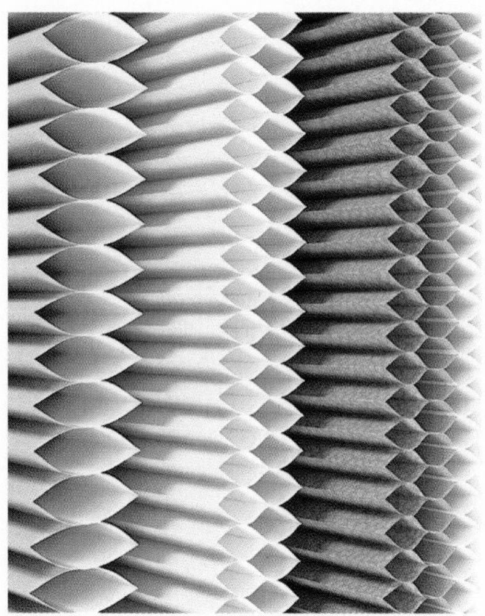

Cellular shades are available with single, double, or—for maximum energy efficiency—triple honeycombs.

Inquire about the warranty for a quality shade. Some professionally installed shades are guaranteed to be free from defects for as long as you own them. If you plan to install a shade yourself, see page 102 for some tips.

Pleated shades. Most draw up in 1-inch pleats, though larger and smaller sizes are also sold. Typically all-polyester, the shades come in many colors, textures, and fabric styles, including lace, antique satin, and faux marble. Some designs cater to kids.

Light options range from sheer to opaque. Some shades have two separate fabrics, one translucent and one opaque, with separate pull cords on the same shade so you can switch between the two. Other shades have a thin metallic backing to reflect damaging sunlight.

Attached to a metal headrail, pleated shades are usually pulled by a cord into a compact stack at the top of the window. For special situations, you can get shades that stack at the bottom or unfold from both the top and the bottom to meet in the middle. For side-by-side windows or sliding patio doors, more than one shade can be attached to the headrail and operated independently. Shades can also be custom-fitted to odd-shaped windows such as semicircles and angle-tops as well as skylights; for the latter, the shade runs on tracks and is crank-operated or motorized.

Cellular shades. These single-, double-, and triple-celled shades, with their honeycomb design, evolved from the plain pleated shade and are used in much the same way. Their main advantage is energy efficiency, since the pockets trap air. But don't expect a cellular shade to solve your energy problems if your window is drafty and

A colorful cloud shade provides just the right playful touch in a young child's room.

you keep the shade raised or allow light gaps.

Pleat sizes range from ⅜ to 2 inches, and color and texture options are constantly increasing. Light choices range from sheer to opaque. Like plain pleated shades, some cellular ones have a dual-light option, switching from a translucent to an opaque material on the same shade. Also like pleateds, you can get ones that stack at the bottom or meet in the middle. Some cellular shades that stack at the top are cordless: you just push up or pull down on the bottom bar to move the shade.

In addition to being used in standard windows, cellular shades are often custom-fitted to angle-top, arched, and other odd-shaped windows. They can also be used in the same way as pleated shades in skylights. Though cellular shades are almost always set horizontally, they can be positioned vertically, as they sometimes are on sliding glass doors.

Roller shades. Used alone or in conjunction with other window treatments that are sheer or don't cover the entire window, roller shades provide privacy and block light when pulled down, but they are unobtrusive when rolled up.

If you want a reverse roll (the shade pulls down from the front of the roller), you must specify it. A reverse roll hides the roller and allows an inside-mount shade to sit flush with the window casing.

The operating mechanism is either a standard spring roller or a bead chain, which stops the shade in any position. A bead chain keeps the shade cleaner since you touch only the chain and not the fabric. The chain also makes it easy to raise and lower heavy or hard-to-reach shades.

Custom roller shades are usually made from cotton, linen, or other tightly woven fabrics. Much of their appeal rests in the choice of a decorative hem and shade pull.

Most stock shades are vinyl. Several companies offer inexpensive shades that you can easily size yourself to fit a window. Just slide the adjustable roller to your window's width, strip off excess shade material (tear along scoring in the vinyl), and press the material to the roller. Some brands are plain white, while others offer some choice in color and pattern.

Soft fabric shades. This category includes diverse shade styles. One type is the stagecoach, a custom shade that you roll up by hand and secure with ties. More common are ones that draw up with the aid of cords strung through rings on the back of the shade. With some, the pull cord locks

All the various kinds of Roman shades draw up, like these two, in folds.

the shade at the desired height; with others, you stop the shade by winding the cord around a cleat. These familiar kinds include Roman shades, which draw up into neat horizontal folds; Austrian shades (scalloped folds); and balloon and cloud shades (billows).

Many suppliers offer variations of these classic shade types—for example, shades with deep overlapping folds, with a single scallop at the bottom instead of several, or with a flat top and a poufed bottom.

Fabric shades from the companies that make pleated and cellular shades are another possibility. They work like Roman shades, with folds available in several sizes. Be aware that the headrail into which the shade disappears may be bulky and protrude from the window frame.

Woven shades. These shades consist of strips of wood (matchstick shades have very thin strips), natural fibers, reeds, or grasses. You can usually order an optional lining as well as a fabric edging.

Most shades in this category are Roman shades, though some roll up with a cord-and-pulley system. Many of the Roman types require lots of stacking space, so be sure that there's enough room and that the stacked shade can clear the window glass.

When buying woven woods, look for straight-grained, smoothly cut strips; wood that was kiln-dried is warp resistant.

Popular woven shades are available lined or with fabric banding.

Shutters and Shoji Screens

GREAT FRAME-UPS

Both louvered shutters and shoji screens are elegant, time-honored ways to cover windows. Hybrids consisting of standard fold-back shutter frames with translucent decorative glass or woven cane inserts are newcomers to the market.

Shutters

Quality interior shutters with movable louvers for light control can be costly, but they're one window treatment that adds to a home's value.

Traditional shutters have $1\frac{1}{4}$-inch louvers. Plantation shutters have wider louvers—choices range from about $2\frac{1}{2}$ to $4\frac{1}{2}$ inches wide—for more ventilation and a clearer view. Since slats can

become floppy with age, consider a model with an adjustable tension system. Most shutters have tilt bars, but types that work by moving the louvers directly (you flip one to move all the louvers on a panel) are also sold.

Shutters can be custom-fitted for arched and other odd-shaped windows; they're also available for French doors and sliding patio doors. Horizontal louvers are traditional, but louvers can also be set vertically.

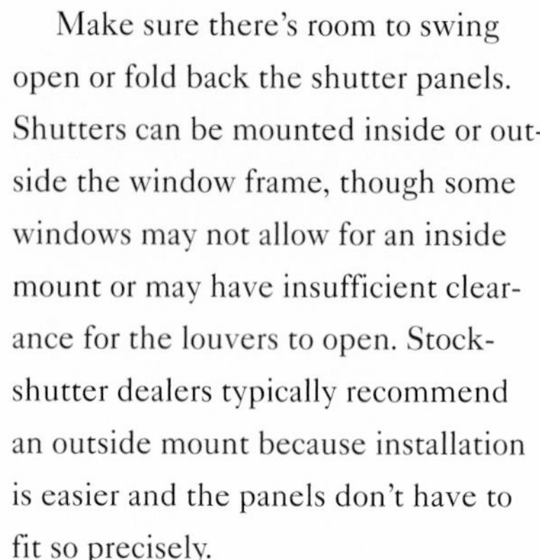

Make sure there's room to swing open or fold back the shutter panels. Shutters can be mounted inside or outside the window frame, though some windows may not allow for an inside mount or may have insufficient clearance for the louvers to open. Stock-shutter dealers typically recommend an outside mount because installation is easier and the panels don't have to fit so precisely.

Quality custom shutters are almost always professionally installed; some dealers won't sell the shutters otherwise, as they don't want to be responsible for the consequences of poor installation. For help in installing stock shutters yourself, see page 102.

Custom and stock shutters are available in three materials—solid wood, vinyl laminated on a foam or wood core, and extruded vinyl.

Wood shutters. These offer more options than their synthetic counterparts. In addition to a greater selection of louver widths and frame styles, you can get wood shutters in standard or custom-matched stains or paint colors. Quality wood shutters can be refinished and are worth repairing.

Plantation shutters hung in front of sliding patio doors create a graceful transition between garden room and garden.

Four shoji panels consist of rice paper inserts in cedar frames. When slid to either side, the screens clear the glass on a pair of double-hung windows.

Custom shutters are commonly made from incense cedar (often labeled as cedar) or alder, flexible woods that won't warp or split. Manufacturers also use other hardwoods, including poplar. Basswood makes a satisfactory shutter, though it's best suited to long, thin elements, such as narrow louvers. Stock shutters, sold by the panel in lumberyards and home centers, are typically made from soft, cheap grades of pine.

Don't count on price to distinguish premium from lesser-quality custom shutters. Look for doweled rather than glued joints (two or three dowels per joint signify a solidly constructed shutter). The louvers should be securely fastened to the tilt bar; they should stay open in a breeze but also close tightly. The finish should be smooth, with no paint or stain buildup.

Vinyl laminated shutters. Vinyl is laminated onto a foam or wood core. The durable finish is unaffected by ultraviolet light, is easy to clean, and never needs refinishing.

Just like solid wood shutters, custom-laminated shutters can be made to fit odd-shaped windows. The laminates are limited in color selection (typically white and ivory), louver widths (most commonly 2½ and 3½ inches), and frame styles. A quality product should have tight joints and louvers that hold steady when tilted. Some look more realistic than others, so shop carefully.

Extruded vinyl shutters. These shutters have a cellular or honeycombed interior. They're as durable and maintenance-free as the laminated types, but because they consist of vinyl throughout, there won't be any color change if you nick or cut the surface. Because current technology does not allow panels to be extruded into odd shapes, these shutters are limited to rectangles.

They share the same limitations as the laminates in color, louver width, and frame style. As you would with the laminated models, check for tight joints, steady louvers, and a realistic appearance.

Shoji screens

These custom-made decorative screens consist of translucent inserts in a wood frame. Although often found in place of windows in traditional Japanese homes, where deep overhangs protect the screens, elsewhere shojis are used as a window treatment.

Rice paper is the traditional insert material, but because it tears easily, it has been largely supplanted by fiberglass treated to look similar to rice paper. Eventually, the fiberglass deteriorates in sunlight and must be replaced. Other synthetic materials, many of them from Japan, are also commonly used.

Shoji screens can be made to slide along a wood track or fold over a window like shutters. Several panels can be hinged together and stacked to one side of the window.

Putting Up Shades, Blinds, and Shutters

The supplier of custom shades, blinds, and shutters will usually mount them, but you may want to install inexpensive types yourself—especially if professional installation will cost more than the window covering itself.

First, make sure the window treatment fits in the spot you planned for it. Hold it in place, positioning the headrail or mounting board at the correct height. The treatment shouldn't interfere with any window hardware, such as handles, and shouldn't impede the smooth operation of the window. If it does, try adjusting its position just enough to avoid the problem.

Window treatments, especially heavy ones, must be securely fastened to the window or wall. To choose the right fastener, see page 96.

If you have different brackets for inside and outside mounts, be sure to use the appropriate ones. Since your window frames may not be perfectly square, use a carpenter's level to position the brackets or hinges; then mark the screw holes with a pencil. Drill holes to accommodate the screws or bolts, and securely fasten the brackets or hinges to the mounting surface.

Shades and blinds

Most shades and blinds come with a pair of brackets, and very wide or heavy ones come with additional support brackets. Once you've attached the brackets, the usual next step is to slide the shade or blind onto the bracket or snap it into place.

If you need extra clearance, use shims or projection brackets to hold the treatment away from the wall or window casing. Some blinds and shades, especially those to be mounted on a door or hinged window, also come with hold-down brackets to keep the bottom stationary. Don't use brackets to keep pleated or cellular shades from being windblown, since doing so can twist the shade.

Shutters

Installing inside-mount shutters is tricky if the window isn't perfectly square (use a carpenter's square, as shown at left, to check). To make the panels fit, you'll have to trim or shim them. You'll also need to nail stops (strips of wood) to the inside top and bottom of the window frame to keep the panels from swinging into the glazing and breaking the hinges. If your window is severely out of square, use an outside mount.

With an outside mount, you can either screw the shutter hinges directly to the window casing or attach them to a frame that you build and screw into the casing.

Another way to install shutters is to use a hanging strip; screw it to the jamb for an inside mount, as shown at left, or to the casing for an outside mount. Some companies that market shutter panels sell kits containing hanging strips, hinges, and screws. Or you can buy preassembled shutters that incorporate hanging strips.

Before installing shutters, check window jambs with a carpenter's square. If they're fairly square, you can use an inside mount: attach each shutter to a hanging strip screwed to the jamb.

Blinds

SIMPLE, SLEEK WAYS TO CONTROL LIGHT

With most window coverings, it's all or nothing. When the treatment is drawn over a window, you can't adjust the amount of light that enters. But with both horizontal and vertical blinds, you can tilt the slats to let in the desired amount of light, or you can darken the room completely. The slats stack out of the way when you want the window uncovered.

Stock blinds are fine if you find ones that fit your window opening perfectly. Otherwise, opt for made-to-measure blinds, especially if you want them for an inside mount. Even at custom prices, most blinds are very affordable, especially for standard, rectangular windows. High-quality wood blinds are at the high end of the price range for blinds, but they're still about half the cost of wood shutters. Vertical blinds with fabric vanes can cost as much as wood blinds, depending on the fabric selection.

Some suppliers offer limited warranties; others promise to repair or replace defective blinds for as long as you own them. Warranties don't usually cover normal wear and tear, though. With horizontal blinds, getting a new blind may cost less than replacing a broken slat.

Horizontal blinds

These traditional blinds are suitable for most windows, including arches and other odd shapes. They're also suitable for skylights and for doors (hold-down clips will keep the blind steady when the door swings open or shut). Most blinds are made of metal, vinyl, or wood—types described on page 104. Also available are blinds with tinted polycarbonate plastic slats that are transparent when closed; on some models, the slats become opaque when they're tilted a certain way.

Any horizontal blind is only as good as its operating mechanism. If you have access to display models, give them a workout before deciding on a

Richly grained wood blinds feature 2-inch slats and decorative cloth tapes.

particular product. Make sure the blind opens and closes smoothly and quietly. The slats should tilt uniformly. As you draw the blind, it should remain level and hold in place where you stop it. The hardware should be sturdy and well constructed, with no rough edges.

For room darkening, choose a blind with opaque, reasonably thick slats. Be sure the slats close tightly and there is no gap between the headrail and the top slat. Light will seep through cord holes that are exposed when the slats are closed. Some blind makers get around this problem by making the holes small, or even by eliminating them and looping cords around the slats instead. Other solutions include covering the holes with decorative cloth tapes, positioning small holes near the back of slats so that they're overlapped when the blind is closed, and placing the holes at the far ends of the slats so that they're positioned against the window frame or wall.

The area that you can cover with one blind varies according to the type of blind. To span the desired distance, you may have to put more than one blind on a single headrail. To protect small children, consider blinds without conventional pull cords. Options include automated systems as well as cordless blinds that you operate by lifting up or pulling down the bottom rail. To cut down on blind cleaning, consider a dust-repellent model.

Metal blinds. Typically, metal blinds are made of aluminum alloy with a baked enamel finish; matte finishes are also available. Most makers offer a wide range of colors. Metal blinds come in a variety of slat widths, most commonly 2 inches (Venetian blinds), 1 inch (miniblinds), and ½ or ⅝ inch (micro-miniblinds). In-between slat sizes, such as 1⅜ inches, are also sold. Contrasting cloth tapes are optional with most 2-inch metal blinds.

These sleek vinyl miniblinds are inexpensive but sturdy enough to withstand rough handling.

Vinyl blinds. Like their metal counterparts, these come in a range of slat sizes. Moisture-resistant vinyl blinds are a good choice for bathrooms and kitchens. Low price makes them a favorite window treatment in kids' rooms (most vinyl blinds are now lead-free, but check before buying). Two-inch vinyl blinds have grown in popularity—and price—because of the fashionable textured finishes available; you can coordinate them with cloth tapes.

Wood blinds. In addition to all-wood blinds, this category now includes blinds made of synthetic materials: vinyl laminated onto a wood core and extruded vinyl. Because these blinds can be heavy to raise (the synthetics actually weigh more than real wood slats), keep a single blind to less than about 6 feet wide. Also note that the wider the slat, the fewer the slats there are and the less stacking room is required. Even wide-slat wood blinds need considerable stacking space, so ask before buying.

Solid wood blinds feature slats from 1 inch to about 3 inches wide, in your choice of stain or paint finish (options include washes and faux finishes); coordinating cloth tapes are optional. Manufacturers warn customers to expect some variation in wood grain and color. Look for quality, kiln-dried wood, because it will resist warping.

Makers of synthetic wood blinds usually offer two or three slat widths, and a variety of colors and textured finishes. These blinds are moisture and warp resistant, making them suitable for humid climates and for use in kitchens and bathrooms. They also wear better in extreme temperatures and direct sunlight than blinds made of solid wood.

Vertical blinds

These blinds, which stack compactly to the side, are practical for sliding patio doors and picture windows. They can be used on other types of windows, even bays and odd shapes such as arches. They require less cleaning than horizontal blinds since gravity keeps dust from piling up.

The vertical slats, called vanes, are usually 3½ inches wide, though wider and narrower versions are also sold. The vanes are most commonly made of fabric or vinyl. You can also get vanes of wood, metal, or tinted polycarbonate plastic—the same materials used in many horizontal blinds.

For fabric vanes, choose either free-hanging fabric panels with weighted hems or fabric strips inserted into a grooved backing. Manufacturers have taken fabric vertical blinds a step farther, attaching white fabric vanes to a sheer panel-like face fabric, creating the effect of a curtain when the vanes are open; when you rotate the vanes to a shut position, the sheer curtain becomes opaque. As an alternative, you can "slipcover" existing verticals in sheer panels sold for that purpose; you simply remove the cover to wash the sheers.

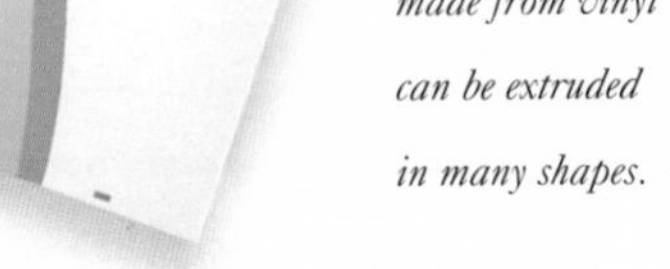

Vertical vanes made from vinyl can be extruded in many shapes.

When closed, these vertical blinds with fabric vanes provide complete privacy.

In addition to plain vinyl vanes in solid colors, you'll find versions that have been extruded in various printed designs and in curves, ridges, and other shapes. You can also get vanes perforated with tiny holes that will filter light without blocking the view.

Operating options include standard cords or a single wand that allows you to rotate the vanes as well as open and close the blind. Motorized vane rotation is also available. Sturdiness is important with vertical blinds: tug on the vanes to make sure the attachment to the headrail is secure. Because hangers holding the vanes can break, find out if they're replaceable.

A Word to the (Energy) Wise

Most window treatments have an insulating effect, but some do a better job than others at keeping the sun's heat outside in summer and heated air inside in winter. Depending on your situation, you may want window coverings that are efficient during hot weather or cold weather, or in both situations.

Remember, there's no point in having energy-wise treatments unless they're shielding your windows at the critical times. During hot months, close the treatments early in the day before the temperature soars; in cold weather, draw them at sunset.

Cool in summer

You may find that some rooms, especially those facing south or west, become uncomfortably hot in summer. Shutters and blinds (both horizontal and vertical) do a good job of barring heat, as do cellular shades (double- and triple-celled shades trap more heat than single-celled types).

Choose white or metallic backings on treatments to reflect sunlight away from the windows. The materials used in some window coverings will also protect against ultraviolet rays, which can fade the contents of a room.

Toasty in winter

The following are some treatment types as well as strategies to help prevent heat from escaping your home's interior during the cold season.

Insulating, snug-fitting shades bar the sun's rays in summer and keep heated air from escaping in winter.

Among the most energy-efficient treatments are cellular shades (double- and triple-celled types do a better job than those with single cells), shutters, and quilted Roman shades. Remember, inside-mount shades must fit snugly within the frame if they are to be effective.

Layered treatments—for example, heavy draperies with sheers next to the glass or curtains with a pleated shade underneath and topped by a cornice or valance—also inhibit heat loss. Curtains and draperies that extend well beyond the window, perhaps from the ceiling to the floor and at least several inches on either side of the window, do a considerably better job of shielding against heat loss than ones that cover more skimpily.

Linings can greatly increase the energy efficiency of draperies and other fabric window treatments. In addition to linings made of standard cotton and cotton-polyester blends, you can order energy-efficient insulating and/or blackout linings. Interlinings provide even more insulation. (For more about the various types of linings, see page 87.)

If you have older windows that leak a little, try sealing the edges of the window treatment with hook-and-loop fastening tape, commonly available at fabric stores.

Top Treatments

CROWNING GLORIES FOR YOUR WINDOWS

Top treatments are providing much of the excitement in today's window fashions. The treatment can sit above the window, or it can frame the top and sides. You can use it alone as an accent on an uncovered window or, where privacy is an issue, combine it with curtains, shades, or other window coverings.

The most common toppers are cornices, valances, swags, and scarves, described below. Other types of embellishment can consist of simple wood poles that you cover in fabric, or elaborate molded architectural accent pieces available through decorators.

This painted wood cornice conceals the tops of undertreatments, while adding panache.

An easy way to hang a swag or scarf is to thread it through decorative brackets positioned at the upper corners of a window.

Cornices

This is a shallow, boxlike frame installed across the top of a window. (If the frame has legs that extend to the floor, it is called a lambrequin.) The frame projects out from the window, hiding a curtain or drapery heading or the tops of any other undertreatments.

Cornices are traditionally built of wood, then padded and upholstered in fabric. Modern ready-made versions are often constructed of molded polystyrene or other lightweight materials, usually with facades that resemble oversized crown molding. The frame is closed at the top to keep dust away from any undertreatments. Manufacturers typically offer these frames in a couple of colors and in several widths and heights, to about 9 inches high. They suggest customizing the cornice by adding paint, wallpaper, fabric, or rubber-stamp impressions, or by gluing on decorative objects for a three-dimensional look.

As an alternative to the standard frame, you can make your own shallow cornice (to about 4½ inches high) from a wide-pocket rod. Just snap on the manufacturer's optional foam fascia, then cover with fabric.

Valances

This type of fabric top treatment may be flat, pleated, or gathered and hung from a rod, pole, or board. A simple valance that you can make yourself is a short fabric panel with a heading that you shirr onto a wide-pocket rod (minus the fascia) or one with tab tops that you thread onto a pole.

You can find ready-made valances in many styles, including ones with bottoms that are arched, scalloped, pointed, pleated, or poufed, as well as types with tails that drape down the sides of the window. Some valances consist of a single panel, while others have two panels; for the latter, an insert valance (a middle piece) is sometimes sold for wider windows.

Scarves and swags

These are pieces of fabric that you drape artfully over the top of the window and down the sides—you may decide to stop partway down the window or go all the way to the floor.

Though the terms are sometimes used interchangeably, a scarf consists of a single piece of fabric and a swag of several pieces joined together. The reason for forming a swag from more than one piece is so that it will drape in a characteristic curved shape. Rather than have swags sewn, decorators often just pin pieces of fabric until they find a shape that works, then staple them neatly together. The same suppliers who offer curtain and drapery panels also sell scarves and swags that are ready for draping.

Draping scarves and swags attractively takes some time and expertise, though various tools and techniques will help you. Assorted decorative brackets, including those labeled "scarf holder," "swag holder," or "sconce," are popular for securing the fabric at the top corners of the window; use an extra holder in the middle for wide windows. Just thread the fabric through the holders, or drape it over their tops. You can use the holders with or without a pole or rod. Holdbacks are another type of hardware that you can use to secure long scarves or cascades at the sides of windows. In addition to serving an important function, the various hardware pieces add beautiful decorative accents to the window. (For more about these, see pages 92–93.)

Another simple approach is to install a pole or rod, then loosely wrap a scarf around it or anchor a swag to it. You can staple fabric to a wooden pole to keep it in place. Some manufacturers of window-treatment hardware produce special rubber pads for pinning fabric to metal rods.

The hardware makers also turn out plastic templates, some of them labeled "design rings," to help you form poufs or rosettes, or arrange fabric artistically in other ways. With valance pleaters (notched plastic that you install at the top corners of the window), you can drape fabric in addition to forming valances.

Gathered valances trimmed with oversize contrasting welt are color-coordinated with window-seat cushions and pillows.

Care and Cleaning

Your window coverings will look better and last longer if they're cared for properly. Follow the manufacturer's instructions for care and cleaning; also refer to the tips below.

■ Some draperies and Roman or Austrian shades need "dressing" to train them into pleats or folds. Smooth the fabric into place by hand as you draw the draperies or raise the shades. Eventually, the treatment will form precise pleats or folds on its own. For an easy way to train draperies, see the illustration at right.

■ Most curtains and draperies should be dry-cleaned rather than washed, but do so infrequently as harsh chemicals can harm some fabrics. Even if the decorative face fabric withstands chemical cleaning, a lining weakened by exposure to the sun may come back in shreds.

To lengthen the intervals between dry cleanings, vacuum often to remove dirt that might otherwise be absorbed over time. Once or twice a year, tumble the panels in the clothes dryer. To avoid removing drapery hooks, secure the hem over the hooks with safety pins. Add a dry, all-cotton terry-cloth towel to absorb dirt and, unless the fabric contains polyester, a fabric softener sheet. Set the dryer on "no heat" or "air fluff" and run it for about 30 minutes. Remove and hang the curtains or draperies immediately; you may have to iron or steam them to get wrinkles out. Panels cared for in this manner should look good for years without dry cleaning.

To train draperies, open the panels completely. With your fingers, smooth the fabric into pleats or folds, and then tie them in place with soft fabric strips. After a few days, remove the ties.

For washable curtains (if the fabric has been preshrunk), hand-wash one panel at a time in sudsy water that is comfortably hot to the touch. Drain the water as soon as it turns dirty, then rinse. Wash and rinse again. Hang to dry; touch up with an iron if needed.

■ Keep shades clean by vacuuming them often. To remove a stain from a pleated or cellular shade, lightly sponge the area with mild detergent and lukewarm water. When the shades begin to look soiled or dowdy, ultrasonic cleaning is a good way to spruce them up (see at right). Check the manufacturer's instructions for the proper way to clean other types of shades.

■ Keep horizontal or vertical blinds looking fresh by dusting them with a clean, soft cloth or vacuuming with a soft brush attachment. To clean both surfaces, go over the blinds with the slats tilted one way and then the other, but not completely closed. To avoid scratching polycarbonate plastic blinds, use a very soft cloth and an extremely diluted, mild detergent or a cleaner recommended for computer screens. To keep stained wooden blinds in good condition, dab furniture oil on the cloth when you dust.

For do-it-yourself cleaning of metal or vinyl blinds, use a damp cloth and mild detergent, then wipe dry immediately to prevent spotting. You can immerse vinyl blinds in the bathtub, but dunking metal blinds can cause rusting. For professional cleaning of blinds, consider ultrasonic cleaning.

■ Many window treatments can be ultrasonically cleaned, the same kind of process used for cleaning jewelry. The solution in which the treatment is immersed contains tiny sound-wave–generated bubbles that knock dirt loose. Pleated and cellular shades—as well as horizontal and vertical blinds made of metal, vinyl, plastic, fabric, or wood—can be cleaned in this fashion.

design credits

FRONT MATTER

1. Interior designer: Katherine Hill Interiors. Window treatment: Poppy Design Service. Furniture and bedding: Jonathan Kaye. 2. Interior designer: Juvenile Lifestyles, Inc./Norm Claybaugh. 4. Interior designer: Lisa DeLong/DeLong Designs & Interiors. 5 (top). Interior designer: Frank Van Duerm Design Associates. 5 (bottom). Interior designer: Katherine Hill Interiors.

A PLANNING PRIMER

6. Interior designer: Claire L. Sommers/McCabe & Sommers Interiors.

Window Wear

8. Interior designer: Janice L. McCabe/McCabe & Sommers Interiors. 9 (both). Interior designer: Osburn Design. 10. Interior designer: Paulette Trainor. 11 (top). Design: "idea house" at San Francisco Design Center. 11 (middle). Interior designer: Richard Witzel & Associates. 11 (bottom). Design: Summer House at One Ford Road, Newport Beach, by Pacific Bay Homes. 12 (top). Interior designer: Lisa DeLong/DeLong Designs & Interiors. 12 (bottom). Interior designer: Suzanne Tucker/Tucker & Marks. Architects: Hunt, Hale & Associates. 14 (top). Interior designer: Claire L. Sommers/McCabe & Sommers Interiors. 14 (bottom). Interior designer: Elizabeth Benefield. 15 (top). Interior designer: Marilyn Riding Design. 15 (bottom). Design: Japan Woodworking & Design. 16 (top). Design: Summer House at One Ford Road, Newport Beach, by Pacific Bay Homes. 16 (bottom). Interior designer: Elizabeth Hill of Selby House Ltd. Window treatment: Rossetti & Corriea Draperies. 17 (top). Interior designer: Janice L. McCabe/McCabe & Sommers Interiors. 17 (bottom). Interior designer: Katherine Hill Interiors. 18 (right). Interior designer: Susan McKeehan. 19 (right). Architect: Richardson Architects. 19 (left). Design: Jan Tetzlaff, Arabesque.

Design Decisions

20 (left). Interior designer: Tres McKinney of Laura Ashley. 20 (right). Interior designer: Joan Neville Designs. 21 (left). Interior designer: Interiors by Lindsay Steenblock and Susan McKeehan. 21 (right). Design: Summer House at One Ford Road, Newport Beach, by Pacific Bay Homes. 22. Interior designer: Cathleen Waronker and Mellissa Dietz. 23 (left). Design: Michelle Green. Fabrics: Calico Corners. 23 (right). Interior designer: Lisa DeLong/DeLong Designs & Interiors. 24 (left). Interior designer: Lindsay Steenblock/County Clare Design. 24 (right). Interior designer: Tres McKinney of Laura Ashley. 25 (both). Design: "idea house" at San Francisco Design Center.

Practical Matters

26. Interior designer: Paulette Trainor. 27. Interior designer: Frank Van Duerm Design Associates.

GREAT WINDOW TREATMENTS

34. Interior designer: Susan Federman & Marie Johnston Interior Design.

Curtain Call

36 (top). Interior designer: David Dalton Associates. 36 (bottom). Interior designer: Paulette Trainor. 37 (top). Interior designer: Agins Interiors. 37 (bottom). Interior designer: Richard Witzel & Associates.

Sheer Simplicity

38 (top). Design: Summer House at One Ford Road, Newport Beach, by Pacific Bay Homes. 38 (bottom). Interior designer: Bauer Interior Design. 39. Interior designer: Peter R. Baty. 40. Interior designer: Ruth Livingston Interior Design. 41 (top). Interior designer: Jay Jeffers. 41 (bottom). Interior designer: Jay Jeffers/Richard Witzel & Associates. 42–43 (all). Designer/decorative painter: Peggy Del Rosario. 44 (top). Window Treatment: Rossetti &

Corriea Draperies. 44 (bottom). Interior designer: Dominique Sanchot Stenzel—La Belle France. Builder: Godby Construction, Inc. 45. Interior designer: Agnes Bourne, Inc.

Versatile Shades
46 (top). Interior designer: Richard Witzel & Associates. 46 (bottom). Interior designer: Tres McKinney of Laura Ashley. 47 (top). Interior designer: Dominique Sanchot Stenzel—La Belle France. Builder: Godby Construction, Inc. 47 (bottom). Interior designer: Richard Witzel/Richard Witzel & Associates. 48. Interior designer: Dianna V. 49 (middle right). Interior designer: Monty Collins Interior Design and Willem Racké Studio. 49 (bottom). Design: Layne Gray. 50–51. Interior designer: Richard Witzel & Associates. 51 (top). Interior designer: Amy Weaver of Weaver Design Group. Decorative painter: Page Kelleher. 51 (bottom). Interior designer: J. van Doorn Design.

Billowy Clouds
52. Interior designer: Lisa DeLong/DeLong Designs & Interiors. 53 (top). Interior designer: George Davis Interiors. 53 (bottom). Interior designer: Elizabeth Hill of Selby House Ltd. Window treatment: Rossetti & Corriea Draperies.

Shutters and Shojis
54. Design: Japan Woodworking & Design. 55 (top). Design: Summer House at One Ford Road, Newport Beach, by Pacific Bay Homes. 55 (bottom). Design: smith +noble windowware.

Top Treatments
56 (top). Interior designer: Claire L. Sommers/McCabe & Sommers Interiors. 56 (bottom). Window treatment: Sharon Williams. Furniture: Bellini for Babies & Children. Muralist: Janet White. 57. Interior designer: Colienne Brennan. 58. Interior designer: Leavitt/Weaver, Inc. 59. Interior designer: Richard Witzel & Associates. 60 (both). Interior designer: Janice L. McCabe/ McCabe & Sommers Interiors. 61. Interior designer: Tres McKinney of Laura Ashley. 62–63. Interior designer: Monty Collins Interior Design. 63. Interior designer: Geoffrey De Sousa/de sousa hughes. 64. Interior designer: Janice L. McCabe/McCabe & Sommers Interiors. 65 (top). Window treatment: Cindy Lorensen. 66. Window treatment: Rossetti & Corriea Draperies. 67 (top). Window treatment: Rossetti & Corriea Draperies. 67 (bottom). Interior designer: Elizabeth Hill of Selby House Ltd. Window treatment: Rossetti & Corriea Draperies.

Pattern Play
68 (top). Interior designer: Richard Witzel & Associates. 68 (bottom). Interior designer: Joan Neville Designs. 69: Interior designer: Lindsay Steenblock/County Clare Design.

Yellow Is Primary
70 (left). Interior designer: Diane Kremer/Kremer Design Group. 71. Interior designer: Suzanne Tucker/ Tucker & Marks. Architects: Hunt, Hale & Associates.

Window Seats
72 (top). Interior designer: Geoffrey De Sousa/de sousa hughes. 72 (left). Interior designer: Lindsay Steenblock/County Clare Design. 72 (bottom). Interior designer: Ann Davies Interiors. 73. Interior designer: Elizabeth Hill of Selby House Ltd. Window treatment: Rossetti & Corriea Draperies.

Special Effects
74–75 (all). Interior designer: Osburn Design. 76 (top) Interior designer: City Studios. 76 (bottom). Interior designer: J. van Doorn Design. 76–77. Interior designer: Paulette Trainor.

Not Just for Windows
78. Interior designer: Mel Lowrance. 78 (right and bottom). Interior designer: Ann Welch Design Group. 79 (both). Decorative painter: Peggy Del Rosario.

A SHOPPER'S GUIDE

80. Interior designer: Norm Claybaugh/Juvenile Lifestyles, Inc. Decorative artist: Rebecca. 81. Calico Corners.

Windows
82. Home Depot. 83 (top and middle). Dolan's.

Fabric
84-85. Calico Corners.

Trims
88-89 (bottom). Calico Corners. 89 (top). Design: Mary Cason.

Hardware
90. Conso Products Co., Rue de France (www.ruefrance@efortress.com), smith+noble windoware (www.smithandnoble.com). 91. Conso Products Co. 92 (top). Calico Corners. 92 (bottom). Rue de France, smith+noble windoware. 93. Conso Products Co., Ikea, Restoration Hardware (www.restorationhardware.com), smith+noble windoware.

Ready-made Panels
94. smith+noble windoware. 95 (top panel). Restoration Hardware.

Shades
98. Interior Designer: Elizabeth Hill/Selby House. 99. (top). The Roman Shade Co. 99. (bottom). smith+noble windoware, Maxwell Window Shades, San Francisco., The Roman Shade Co.

Shutters and Shoji Screens
100 (top). San Francisco Shutter Co. 101. Interior designer: Jan Higgins. Window treatment: Hana Shoji & Interiors.

Blinds
103, 104, 105 (bottom). smith+noble windoware. 105 (top). Beauti-Vue Products.

A Word to the (Energy) Wise
106. Window treatment: Muffy Hook.

Top Treatments
107 (top). Interior designer: Janice L. McCabe/McCabe & Sommers Interiors. 107 (bottom). Bracket: smith+noble windoware. Swag design and fabrication: Lynne Tremble. 108. Window treatment: Muffy Hook.

DESIGN CREDITS

110. Interior designer: Elizabeth Benefield. 111. Window treatment: Mara Rigel.

PHOTOGRAPHERS

Unless noted, all photographs are by E. Andrew McKinney.

Philip Harvey: 8, 38 (bottom),39, 40, 42–43, 45, 57, 58, 70 (left), 74–75, 78 (all), 83 (bottom), 100 (bottom), 106, 108. Colin McRae: 97. John O'Hagan: 5 (left). Tom Wyatt: 19 (bottom).

index

Page numbers in **boldface** refer to photographs